talking PICTURES

Pictorial texts and young readers

Edited by Victor Watson and Morag Styles

Hodder & Stoughton

A MEMBER OF THE HODDER HEADLINE GROUP

British Library Cataloguing in Publication Data

Talking Pictures
  I. Watson, Victor II. Styles, Morag
  372.4

ISBN 0–340–64821–X

First published 1996
Impression number   10 9 8 7 6 5 4 3 2 1
Year   1999   1998   1997   1996

Typeset by Wearset, Boldon, Tyne & Wear
Printed in Great Britain for Hodder & Stoughton Educational, a division of Hodder Headline Plc, 338 Euston Road, London NW1 3BH by Redwood Books, Trowbridge, Wilts

Contents

Acknowledgements   v

The contributors   vi

Introduction – A variety of voices   1

1   Pop-ups and fingle-fangles: the history of the picture book   5
David Lewis

2   Inside the tunnel: a radical kind of reading – picture books, pupils and post-modernism   23
Morag Styles

3   Tricks and treats: picture books and forms of comedy   48
Barbara Jordan

4   Reading picture books with an artist's eye   61
Helen Gomez-Reino

5   Getting into the picture   71
Shirley Hughes

6   Imaginationing Granpa: journeying into reading with John Burningham   80
Victor Watson

7   Spying on picture books: exploring intertextuality with young children   101
Helen Bromley

8   Her family's voices: one young reader tuning into reading   112
Victor Watson

9   Reading *The Beano*: a young boy's experience   123
Michael Rosen

10   'Madam! Read the scary book, Madam' – the emergent bilingual reader   136
Helen Bromley

11   The left-handed reader: linear sentences and unmapped
     pictures   145
     Victor Watson

12   Penny plain, tuppence coloured: reading words and pictures   164
     Helen Arnold

Conclusion – a final word   178

Index   182

Acknowledgements

Victor Watson and Morag Styles would like to express their gratitude to Shirley Hughes for her help throughout the preparation of this book and particularly for her cooperation in the design of the cover.

The editors and publisher would also like to thank the following for permission to reproduce material in this book:
Shirley Hughes for illustrations from *Up and Up*, copyright © 1979 Shirley Hughes on pages 39 and 40; André Deutsch Children's Books for the illustration from *Jyoti's Journey*, copyright © 1986 Helen Ganley on page 62; Walker Books for the illustration from *Piggybook*, copyright © 1986 Anthony Browne on page 64; Random House UK Limited/Philomel for the illustration from *Anno's Journey*, copyright © 1977 Mitsumasmo Anno on page 65; Andersen Press for the illustration from *Angry Arthur*, copyright © 1982 Satoshi Kitamura, on page 67; Penguin for the illustration from *The True Story of the Three Little Pigs*, copyright © 1989 Jon Scieszca and Lane Smith on page 69; Shirley Hughes for the sample rough illustrations for a forthcoming project on pages 76, 77 and 78; Jonathan Cape/Random House UK and Crown Publishers, Inc. for the illustrations from *Granpa*, copyright © 1984 John Burningham on pages 82, 83, 84, 89, 92, 93, 120; Jonathan Cape/Random House UK for the illustration from *Come away from the water, Shirley*, copyright © 1977 John Burningham on page 96; Walker Books for the illustrations from *The Tunnel*, copyright © 1989 Anthony Browne on pages 114, 149 and 153; Jonathan Cape/Random House UK and Crown Publishers, Inc. for the illustration from *Aldo*, copyright © 1991 John Burningham on page 120; Reed Consumer Books for the illustrations from the *The Hobyahs*, copyright © 1977 Simon Stern on page 139; The Bodley Head/Random House UK for the illustration from *Rosie's Walk*, copyright © 1968 Pat Hutchins on page 152; Walker Books for the illustration from *Look What I've Got*, copyright © 1980 Anthony Browne on page 156; Walker Books for the illustration from *Gorilla*, copyright © 1983 Anthony Browne on page 159; Jonathan Cape/Random House UK and Henry Holt & Co. Inc. for the illustration from *Mr Gumpy's Outing*, copyright © 1971 John Burningham on page 160; Jonathan Cape/Random House UK and HarperCollins USA for the illustration from *Avocado Baby*, copyright © 1982 John Burningham on page 170; Heinemann Educational for the illustration from *Silly Billys*, copyright © 1988 Joy Cowley on page 168.

Every effort has been made to trace and acknowledge ownership of copyright. The publishers will be glad to make suitable arrangements with any copyright holders whom it has not been possible to contact.

The contributors

· ·

Helen Arnold is a key name in reading and education. As author of *Listening to Children Reading* she is widely respected and much in demand as a lecturer on literacy. Previously a teacher educator, researcher, and advisor for English, in recent years she has developed a rich freelance career as a speaker, consultant and writer. One of her current interests is in non-fiction reading and writing.

Helen Bromley worked in Essex schools for many years and was Deputy Head at Sunnymede Infant School when she decided to shift to a freelance career, including teaching students at Homerton College. Her commitment to children learning to read with 'real books' has won her public recognition: she has featured in television programmes, is in demand as a speaker and is busy with a number of writing projects.

Helen Gomez-Reino completed her BEd in Fine Art and Education at Homerton College in 1994. Her fascination for picture books was sparked off by a tripos course on children's literature in her final year. She has begun her teaching career in Spain where she plans to develop her interest in art and literacy.

Shirley Hughes has an international reputation as an outstanding author of picture books for children. Mention titles such as *Dogger*, one of the *Alfie* books or *Up and Up* to children or adults and see the delighted response. Of her many talents, it is worth highlighting her devotion to her young audience, the quality of her draughtsmanship and her willingness to reflect on her work and explain her thinking to non-artists.

Barbara Jordan taught in London primary schools for many years as teacher and Headteacher, before she joined the staff at Homerton College as Director of Curriculum and Professional Studies. She has recently moved to the north of England to work as an Inspector for English where she is able, amongst other things, to pursue her interest in picture books and their young readership.

David Lewis is a Lecturer in English at the University of Exeter. He must be one of the first people in the country to have completed a PhD on picture books. We are very lucky that he has allowed us to draw on his extensive research, suitably adapted by the author, for this volume. He has written many well-received articles on pictorial texts in distinguished books and journals.

Michael Rosen is a well-known author, writer, scholar and broadcaster who has written a great number of books of stories, poetry and forms of humour which are extremely popular with children and teachers. He is also one of the most gifted performers of his own work in the country and is much in demand as a speaker both at schools and conferences. Michael Rosen is also a champion of children's rights and speaks up on their behalf at every opportunity. He is the presenter of programmes such as *Treasure Islands* and has recently begun work on a poetry programme for Radio 3. The fact that he also writes scholarly articles on subjects as diverse as reading *The Beano* and the work of Robert Louis Stevenson, demonstrates his versatility.

Morag Styles is Language Co-ordinator at Homerton College where she teaches literacy and children's literature. She runs writing workshops with children and teachers, compiles anthologies of poetry, reviews poetry for children and writes on aspects of children's literature. Although better known for her work on poetry, she has long been a passionate enthusiast for the picture book. She is currently finishing a book on the history of poetry written for children, entitled *From the Garden to the Street*, and editing [with Chris Powling] a new version of *The Books for Keeps Guide to Poetry.*

Victor Watson is a Principal Lecturer in English at Homerton College, Cambridge. He has a special interest in the history and nature of children's books and their relationship both with adult literature and with changing assumptions about childhood. He has made a close study of books for children in the eighteenth and nineteenth centuries, and he has a particular interest in William Blake, Lewis Carroll and Arthur Ransome.

He has worked closely for many years with reception children learning to read with picture books and has written for *Signal, TES, Cambridge Journal of Education, UKRA Journal* and *Books for Keeps.* He is currently beginning work as the editor of the forthcoming *Cambridge Guide to Children's Books.*

Introduction – A variety of voices

The voices of picture books are intimate and the sharing of them tends towards the conspiratorial. Anyone who has read picture books with very young children knows that they promote personal, detailed and exploratory talk as well as social or even raucous merriment. Such occasions may be touched with the high seriousness and gentleness which young readers are capable of – but the satirical may break in at any moment, and the victim of its ridicule may be the adult reader companion. No one is exempt from the laughter of children.

The title of this book is not arbitrary; *Talking Pictures* is a conversation about picture books. It is concerned with the voices of children and adults who have a special interest in these books. In the world of educational discourse, in classrooms, in libraries and corridors, and in children's bedrooms, picture books generate *talk*.

It is not, we hope, a one-sided conversation. We value the picture book both as an art object and as a central tool in the development of reading. Accordingly, the contributors to this book have things to say about the reading lessons within picture books, about their cultural place and significance, about how they are made, and about how they become part of the lives and learning of young readers.

In Chapter 1 David Lewis refers to picture books as fecund and fantastical. The contributors to *Talking Pictures* share that view and seek to pay tribute to their astonishing versatility. Picture books can make themselves at home anywhere and in any genre – as fairytales, information books, nursery rhymes, counting rhymes, pop-up books, comics, newspapers and nonsense – or they can shamelessly borrow elements from all of these. Their narratives range from the mischievously fantastical to the cosily domestic, and their concerns may be the deepest varieties of human sadness and loss, the bitter social cruelties of poverty and violence, the joyously comforting release of anarchic laughter, or the reassuring themes of a safe home and a loving family. Furthermore, they may adopt all manner of forms, presenting themselves both in popular guises and in the conventions of high art.

Picture books welcome and value private and secret learning, and bring into play a hundred subtle interpreting activities which are not susceptible to testing. They encourage a perpetual readiness for the unexpected in their readers, and welcome and provide for both experienced and inexperienced readers alike. They lure into readings and re-readings, and thus remind older children of the earlier partly-forgotten readers they once were, showing them that they have an unfolding 'literate history'. And they do all these things by valuing the reader and allowing freedom of interpretation.

A picture book welcomes and provides for young readers' detailed observation of image and, as a bonus, supports their developing sight-vocabulary and growing phonic confidence. Who in their right mind could ever have believed that picture books somehow worked against the proper and necessary development of these capacities? Yet it is true that a reader cannot *simply* decode or decipher a picture book. We have come in recent years to understand that central to the picture book is the notion of the readerly gap – that imaginative space that lies hidden somewhere between the words and the pictures, or in the mysterious syntax of the pictures themselves, or between the shifting perspectives and untrustworthy voices of the narratives. And we have come to acknowledge young readers' extraordinary ability to allow their growing wisdom and knowledge of their own lives to inform and shape those gaps of meaning – except that this ability is not extraordinary at all; it is *ordinary*, the ordinary curiosity of young minds weaving together the strands of their lives in search of pattern and meaning.

There is no right way to read picture books. Because they welcome divergent readings, picture books are subversive both of narrative expectations and cultural orthodoxies. Consequently, they are inevitably political – they tend to be concerned with rule-breaking, mischief and challenge. They teach the rules, and at the same time they invoke laughter and subversive questioning. Think about the old reading schemes of the sixties and seventies; they handed meaning over in tidy linear sequences, not only verbal meaning but cultural meanings of obedience and good behaviour. But today's picture books are not about the already-constructed meanings of other people, they are concerned with the moment-by-moment uncertainty of *making* your own meanings.

However, it is not enough to rhapsodise about picture books; the contributors to *Talking Pictures* know that it is important to describe and analyse attentively their characteristics and their educational and cultural significance. Accordingly, this book provides accounts of the sophisticated understandings of which young readers are capable when they engage with challenging pictorial texts, including comics; descriptions of the ways in which picture books may be used in classrooms, particularly in terms of intertextuality and 'multi-layeredness'; and close examination of a number of central picture book texts (by Ahlbergs, Briggs, Browne, Burningham, Hughes, Kitamura, McKee, Ormerod, Sendak, Smith and Scieszka . . .) which we know are popular with children and carefully used by teachers in thousands of classrooms. These issues are considered within the context of a neglected history of popular reading, contemporary critical theory, and debates currently taking place about a National Curriculum which almost entirely ignores pictorial literacy. *Talking Pictures* would be incomplete without an account of the narrative and pictorial dynamics governing the making and design of a picture book. And then we hear, coming as it were from the other direction, the voices of astute young readers.

Everywhere today we are aware that there is concern about the decline of serious reading. Many teachers speak of the difficulty of encouraging in the young an enthusiasm either for the great literary works of the past or for urgently challenging new work currently being written. It seems that anyone who is concerned with the teaching of 'literature' at any level is inevitably aware of having to make an effort, of having to work against overwhelming cultural forces. It seems as if there is a struggle to be undertaken, an inert resistance to be overcome, a great generation or cultural gap to be bridged. Why that should be so – or even whether it is so – is not the concern of this book. But how different it is with picture books and their young readers! Here, there is no gap, no resistance, no struggle. Today's picture books weave themselves seamlessly into the lives and talk of their young readers.

3

Picture books constitute a 'welcomed literature' – and what this generation of welcoming readers will do with their learned literacies as they grow older remains to be seen. It might surprise us all. But in the meantime *Talking Pictures* seeks to understand the significance and the workings of this welcoming and of these apparently almost trouble-free processes of assimilation.

Pop-ups and fingle-fangles: the history of the picture book

David Lewis

··

Talking Pictures begins with an historical account of the ancestry of picture books which, David Lewis argues, come out of three separate but inter-related traditions: the chapbook, toys and games, and caricature and the comic strip. (The role of caricature, comic strip and humour in pictorial texts is also taken up in different ways later on in the book by Barbara Jordan, Michael Rosen and Morag Styles.) Drawing on his many years of pioneering scholarship in this field, David Lewis offers a tantalising glimpse into one or two corners within the history of books for children. He does not believe that the genre of picture books is adequately coupled with, or described alongside, the history of illustrated books. Instead, David Lewis takes us on a fascinating journey through bibliographic popular culture from the seventeenth to the nineteenth century, when chapbook peddlars plied their lively trade in tiny books with large claims. Lewis goes on to suggest that the recent popularity of paper engineering in books for children shares a history with toy theatres, folding books, peep-shows, panoramas and flap-books. Finally, Lewis reminds us that many of the best illustrators for children in the Victorian period were also cartoonists, another continuity with the strip-cartoon text of the late twentieth century.

Anyone interested in picture books cannot help but notice what a fecund, sprawling, fantastical form it is. A browse through the children's section of any respectable bookshop quickly reveals how varied and flexible the form seems to be. Such a browse might turn up, amongst other things, folk-tales and alphabets, animal tales and counting books, fantasies and domestic dramas. It would also reveal just how inadequately genre categories such as these map on to the books that we might find. We could just as well list the ways picture book makers toy with the physical form of the book, and would thus come across books with moving parts, books with holes in the pages and with flaps to lift, books in different shapes and sizes, and books that make electronic noises when buttons are pressed. We might also find a wide range of approaches to theme, from the sentimental through the moralistic to the parodic, and we would also undoubtedly find examples of hybrid texts where two or more genres or types are merged within one book.

This high degree of variety and flexibility seems to me to be glaringly obvious and just as glaringly in need of explanation. How did the picture book get to be this way? Is it a late twentieth-century development or have picture books always been like this? At the moment I can find no clear answers to these questions in the literature on children's books and even the histories – the very texts we might expect to be most helpful – provide little in the way of illumination. The reasons for this weakness are interconnected and deeply rooted. To begin with, very little work has been dedicated solely to the emergence and development of the picture book. There is broad agreement on many of the facts and events but in the main they have to be sifted from works addressing larger themes – either the development of book illustration in general or children's book illustration in particular. The most authoritative account we have at present of the development of the children's picture book in England is Brian Alderson's extended essay *Sing a Song for Sixpence: The English Picture Book Tradition and Randolph Caldecott*[1] which was published to accompany an exhibition mounted in 1986 to mark the centenary of Randolph Caldecott's death.

The result of picture books having been embedded within the category of illustrated books is that the two types of text are often inadequately differentiated. The distinction between them is generally understood but is rarely, if ever, acted upon. Whalley and Chester[2] make one of the clearest attempts to mark out the difference

‘ While illustrations are not always necessary or desirable in children's novels they are *an essential part of the picture book* and are usually treated as the most important part, although *the more rewarding examples of the genre show a complete integration of text and illustration*, the

book shaped and designed as a whole, produced by a combination of
finely balanced verbal and visual qualities.   ,
[my emphases]

Thus the best picture books are those where pictures and words are woven
together in some way to produce a composite form of text. The
difficulties appear when the attempt is made to discuss historically
significant exemplars of the form. Consider, for example, the paragraph
that immediately follows the one quoted above

‘ This explosion onto a generally dejected market centred around the publication in 1962 of Brian Wildsmith's **ABC**, which *glowed in colours
brighter than any seen before*, and, with its immediate successors, represented his fullest creative expression. It was *beautifully printed* in Austria
by offset litho, and displayed an *inventive use of both shape and design*,
each page *striking the eye* with different *combinations of colour* and little
white to be seen, in complete contrast to the sparse economies of the
'40s. He followed up this success with, among others, **Birds** (1967) and
Fishes (1968) both of which make good use of *double page spread
bleeds in full colour*.[3]   ,
[my emphases]

The emphasis here, as elsewhere in Whalley and Chester, is clearly upon
the visual appearance of the book alone, and upon the aesthetic qualities
of the pictures, despite the fact that 'balance' and 'integration' of text and
illustration are held to be central to the picture book.

Whalley and Chester are not alone in this strange separation of
exhortation and practice. We find exactly the same problem in other
histories of illustration and, indeed, in Alderson's *Sing a Song for
Sixpence*.[4] The main reason for this slippage from assertions about the
composite nature of the picture book to discussions of the pictures alone
is the wholesale adoption of an art-critical discourse within which the
history is framed. Words and phrases such as, 'charming', 'stylish', 'firm
outlines', 'flat colours', 'russet-tinted', 'textured colour', 'subdued tones',
'soft, decorative shapes', 'single point of vision', 'profile drawing', and so
on abound in the histories. Such terms have the irresistible effect of
drawing attention only to the pictures. They thus assume a viewer

concerned with pictorial images rather than one concerned with overall textual meanings. Picture books are dissolved in this medium only to be reconstituted as books of pictures.

A further difficulty, arising directly out of the emphasis upon the pictorial, is an over-riding concern with the aesthetically fine. Many histories appear to be relatively straightforward chronicles, detailing when books were published, who published them and who influenced whom. But lying beneath this apparently value-free enterprise is usually an assumption that a canon of fine, exemplary works can, and should be identified. The problem here is that this approach cannot cope with the popular, the vulgar, the aesthetically crude and what most writers are prone to refer to as the 'gimmicky'. As a result, much material important to a balanced interpretation of the development of the picture book is swept aside as irrelevant, marginal, or beyond the writer's remit.

As if this were not damaging enough to the enterprise of historical interpretation, there is an obsession with an apparently perpetual decline in standards, a concern that will be depressingly familiar to all teachers of English. Muir[5] quotes a German schoolmaster who, as far back as 1787, was bewailing the fact that at the Leipzig book fair, 'there [were] few pearls and little amber, but much mud, and, at best, painted snail shells.' Slythe[6] finds a 'deplorable decline in standards' in the nineteenth century, and, more recently, Moss[7] is much troubled by the apparent dominance of the children's book market by pop-ups, game books and puzzle books. Given two centuries of decline it is amazing that we have anything worth reading at all.

Current histories fail us, I believe, because they inadequately differentiate between picture books and other forms of illustrated text; they are only able to address themselves to the development of the pictures in picture books; and lastly, they are too much concerned with the aesthetically fine and with the existence of a putative canon. How then might we begin to prepare a better account? In this chapter I discuss three important influences on the development of the picture book which help us to see more clearly how the form has come to be as it is, and which go some way to restoring to the centre ground important phenomena that are often passed over quickly and sometimes even ignored. These influences are the chapbook, the development of toys and games in the nineteenth century, and the rise of caricature.

The chapbook

The chapbook belongs to the prehistory of the picture book and many writers testify to the persistent and vigorous influence of the chapbook tradition upon the picture book as it developed throughout the nineteenth and into the twentieth centuries. In their day chapbooks were immensely popular and would have been found in many homes. They were sold by, and caught their name from, chapmen or pedlars, who travelled the country carrying with them a wide range of artefacts which ordinary folk would find useful or attractive. Darton[8] refers to chapmen as 'the peripatetic village shop'. They were a common sight in seventeenth and eighteenth century Britain and their wares were still being peddled in the nineteenth century.

Chapbooks were generally crudely produced with relatively short texts and simple woodcut illustrations. They were usually very small, about ten centimetres by six, and most often sixteen pages in length. Sometimes they were sold uncut as a single sheet so that buyers might fold, stitch and cut the pages themselves. The brevity and relative simplicity of chapbook texts meant that they could be read and understood by a very wide range of the populace. Thus the scantily educated poor – both adults and children – would have read them and there is ample evidence to suggest that chapbooks also found their way into the hands of the middle classes. Dr Johnson and Wordsworth knew them, and Pepys had them bound in his library.

Subject matter was astonishingly varied and included romances, folk-tales, books of recipes, religious works, household manuals, jokebooks, books of prophecy, ABCs, nursery rhymes, adaptations of early novels such as *Gulliver's Travels* and *Robinson Crusoe*, the final speeches of condemned criminals and much more material of a robust, not to say sensational and scurrilous nature. Much of this material was deemed to be highly unsuitable for children, even though chapbooks produced specifically for young people were common from the middle of the eighteenth century

Figure 1 Four pages from popular early nineteenth-century children's chapbooks, published by two prolific printers, John Kendrew of York and J.G. Rusher of Banbury

> (*i*) From Rusher's *Children in the Wood*, an Historical Ballad
> (*ii*) From Rusher's *Poetic Trifles for Young Gentlemen and Ladies*
> (*iii*) From William Wordsworth's poem *We Are Seven* transposed into a sixteen-page chapbook by Kendrew of York, without acknowledgement and probably without the poet's permission; the book was called *The Little Maid and the Gentleman*; or *We Are Seven*
> (*iv*) From Kendrew's *An Elegy on the Death and Burial of Cock Robin*, showing an early use of the speech-bubble

onwards. They failed the tests of the puritans and their heirs on a number of counts. It was not just that chapbooks could be coarse and ribald; the greater sin was that they offered amusement and excitement at a time when, for many religious folk, reading for pleasure alone was considered sinful.

Moreover, many of the tales were drawn from the oral tradition and dealt with the fanciful themes of romance, folklore and legend. Puritans and later moralists, as well as the followers of Locke and of Rousseau, were united in their condemnation of *Tom Thumb, Jack the Giant Killer* and *Tom Hickathrift*. For Bunyan such tales were all 'fingle-fangle' which ensnared one's soul, whereas Locke, writing at approximately the same time (the end of the seventeenth century) it was 'perfectly useless trumpery'. By the end of the eighteenth century a further cause for concern had arisen in the political turmoil in Europe. The French Revolution generated much anxiety about the stability of the state. Many were fearful that a too rapid spread of literacy would make the populace susceptible to malign political influences through the medium of cheap tracts and material of the chapbook kind. Bob Leeson[9] points out that, 'Far, far worse than Tom Thumb, was Tom Paine.'

Many features of the chapbook were handed on to the earliest picture books, in particular, folkloric themes of all kinds, the chapbook's brevity and composite nature, and its extraordinary flexibility. There is no mystery about this influence for the makers of the earliest proto-picture books had no other models to turn to. At the beginning of the nineteenth century reputable publishers such as Harris and Darton were turning out elegant nursery entertainments based on chapbook models. They borrowed chapbook themes and in many cases simply took over chapbook titles. Harris's first runaway success, *The Comic Adventures of Old Mother Hubbard*, was published in 1805. It reputedly sold ten thousand copies in a few months and was soon joined by a host of similar titles. Chapbook staples such as *Tom Thumb, The Babes in the Wood, Cock Robin, Cinderella, The Fables of Aesop*, and *Jack the Giant Killer* were all reinterpreted as early picture books and many titles were revisited again and again throughout the nineteenth century.

Not only did these early picture books take on chapbook themes wholesale, but to begin with they differed very little in appearance. *Mother Hubbard* is hardly larger than a typical chapbook, it is simply more robust, more carefully produced and possesses rather better illustrations. The key feature, however, is not so much the size but the brevity along with the close integration of text and pictures. Once we recognise this, it is possible to detect the lineaments of the chapbook in much later works. Feaver, for example, astutely points out that

‹ Inevitably . . . *Struwwelpeter* and *The Book of Nonsense* were inspired and shaped to a great extent by the imagery their creators had been brought up on. They are caricatured chapbooks.[10]   ›

Even today it is not at all difficult to see the basic chapbook format lying beneath the sophistications of many modern picture books.

Perhaps the most remarkable feature that the modern picture book has inherited from its chapbook forebears is an extraordinary flexibility. Just as the chapbook could ingest almost anything that came its way, so the picture book seems to be able to assimilate almost any kind of text, allowing for the fact that it is first and foremost a form for young children. This flexibility was evident right from the beginning. Not only did Harris and his competitors publish narrative and folkloric material but they also produced a good deal of pictorialised non-fiction. Alphabets, grammatical primers, punctuation, spelling, counting, geographical and musical themes were all transformed into colourful and entertaining booklets. Even adult pieces such as Cowper's *Diverting History of John Gilpin* and Goldsmith's *Elegy on Mrs Mary Blaize* were successfully pictorialised.

Picture books, play, games and toys

The earliest kinds of picture book were flexible in other ways too, and we see this best in the close association between the emergence of the picture book in the nineteenth century and the burgeoning trade in toys and games. It is a commonplace of children's literature history, and something of a simplification, that a new era in juvenile publishing was inaugurated in 1744 with the publication of John Newbery's *A Little Pretty Pocket-Book*. What is perhaps less well known, however, is that the mid-point of the century also marked a watershed in the invention, manufacture and trade in toys and games. J. H. Plumb, in an introductory essay to Gottlieb[11], points out that whereas there were no toyshops at all in London in 1730, by 1780 they were everywhere, and by 1820 they were big business. Now it is clearly no accident that these two events – the creation of a new form of literature for children on the one hand, and the development of a trade in games and toys on the other – were both happening at the same time. A shift was taking place in the way people felt and thought about children and the accoutrements of childhood, including books and toys, were implicated in this change.

What is of particular interest for students of the picture book is that not only were books and toys linked through the growing belief that play was a legitimate and valuable form of activity for children, but also the association between them was so close that the dividing line separating what constituted books and toys was constantly being blurred. A brief survey of some of the typical products of the time should indicate how quickly books and toys grew together.

The juvenile drama – the enacting of plays at home in miniature toy theatres – first emerged at the beginning of the nineteenth century. Muir[12] cites the claims of a J. K. Green to be the 'Original Inventor and Publisher of Juvenile Theatrical Prints, Established 1808'. By 1812 another publisher by the name of West included the texts of plays in book form so that children could speak the words of the characters as they manipulated the tiny figures. The juvenile drama rapidly became very popular and quickly came to influence the developing picture book. Smith[13] for example, mentions a *Jack the Giant Killer* with a huge folding frontispiece which opens out like a toy theatre proscenium, and Dean and Son brought out a flap-book version of *Cinderella* ('with five set scenes and nine trick changes') in 1880. Theatrical themes, personages and plots, and even some of the physical paraphernalia of the toy theatres, were thus woven into picture book publishing from the start.

A phenomenon closely related to the juvenile drama was the *Peep Show* or *Vista Book*. Peepshows, or gallantry shows, consisting of large boxes on wheels which were pushed around the streets, and which the curious might look into through a peep-hole for a small charge, were popular during the eighteenth century. In the 1820s miniature versions began to appear constructed from printed and cut card which could be folded flat or extended. These perspective views developed into elaborate, telescopic vistas where the illusion of immense distance was created through diminishing theatrical-style flats and the decreasing scale of figures and objects. Popular themes included the Great Exhibition, the proposed Channel Tunnel, scenes in parks and palaces, and versions of court masques.

The technique of zigzag folding also went into the creation of *panoramas*. These zigzag books could be opened out so that all phases and stages of the material within could be viewed at the same time. George Cruikshank's nephew Percy is credited with a memorable version of John Gilpin published in the 1850s, whereas George was himself responsible for several works of this kind including *A Comic Alphabet* and *A Comic Multiplication*. Much later, at the end of 1906, Warne published Beatrix Potter's *The Story of a Fierce Bad Rabbit* and *The Story of Miss Moppet* as zigzag books although they were soon reprinted in the more familiar format. Another form of book-toy developed in the nineteenth century was the Paper Doll. In these highly decorative books the heroes and heroines were depicted in the form of cut-outs in different costumes, each with a space for the head which was supplied separately and which could be inserted in the appropriate place by means of a tab pushed into a slot. According to Muir[14] they were not especially successful as they were expensive to produce and the separate parts were easily lost.

Flap-books – the kind where part-pages or flaps can be lifted to reveal pictures or words beneath – were also invented in the nineteenth century. An early antecedent, probably developed in the late eighteenth century, was the *Harlequinade* or *Turn-up*, a form of picture sheet where developments in the story or theme were concealed by folds in the paper which were turned up one by one. The closest modern equivalent would be the heads, bodies and legs books which allow creatures or human figures to be transformed by turning over part pages.

By the 1840s Dean's were publishing a range of flap-books and other movables. An early piece was *Dame Wonder's Transformations*, a cut-away book where different costumes could be made to fit over the figure of a girl pictured at the end. In the 1850s they were producing *Fairy Tale Scenic Books* where three layers of card on the page could be raised and animated by pulling a ribbon from behind. In the 1860s their *Little Folks Living Nursery Rhymes in Moving Pictures* came with a warning to 'handle with care', a clear indication of the fragility of such works. In the last decades of the century Dean's monopoly in this field was being challenged by German manufacturers and publishers. German colour printing techniques were somewhat in advance of those in Britain and many imaginative and well crafted movables originated there. Lothar Meggendorfer in particular was responsible for elevating the animated figure to extraordinary heights of precision and grace.

When we come to look at how this episode in the development of juvenile publishing and the rise of the picture book is dealt with in the histories what we find is a consistent and persistent tone of disparagement. Time and again the pop-ups, the movables, the peep-shows and the panoramas are herded to one side to make a clear path for the development of the picture book. Interpreted generously this might be seen as a way of sorting out the subject matter, of making clear what is to count as a picture book and what is not. Such an approach, however, distorts the historical record and results in a very lopsided view of what kind of artefact the picture book is. Fortunately not everyone writes from this perspective. Maurice Sendak's *Caldecott & Co.*[15], for example, is a bracing read in this respect, restoring to the foreground figures such as Lothar Meggendorfer. Percy Muir[16] is good, too, in his affection for nineteenth century 'Nick Nacks', as is William Feaver[17] who sees clearly the debt owed by picture books to various aspects of nineteenth century popular culture.

What such writers teach us, and what the record shows, is that picture books have always had the ability to hybridise with and ingest other forms of representation. This is no more than we should expect from a form as flexible as the picture book. We can also see how some of the popular themes derived from the chapbook tradition persisted throughout the nineteenth century and were readily adapted to the picture book's numerous incarnations, often mediated through the conventions of popular theatre. If we resist the temptation to conceive of the picture book as first and foremost a minor art form then we may come to recognise how much its development was influenced by what was popular and fashionable.

Caricature and the comic strip

As it developed throughout the nineteenth century the picture book carried with it the genes of the chapbook and thus retained the brevity and flexibility of that meanest of forms. It also retained some of the chapbook's naughtiness and disrespect and continued to feed into and feed upon popular culture. It was also to gain a huge transfusion of wit, energy, graphic brilliance and narrative drive from the work of cartoonists and caricaturists. Today it is not uncommon for illustrators' names to be almost wholly associated with the picture book, but during the last century picture books tended to be produced by jobbing illustrators who could turn their hands to almost anything and caricature was often their staple fare.

Many of the best known names from the mid-century were as well-known for their cartoons in magazines such as *Punch* and *The Illustrated London News* as they were for their work in book illustration and picture books, 'Alfred Crowquill' (the pseudonym of A. H. Forrester), Richard Doyle, John Leech and Charles Bennett being perhaps the best known. Crowquill began his career under George Cruikshank's guidance and was producing prints and illustrating books (mostly for adults) from the 1820s. It was only later, in the mid-century, that he turned his attention to producing books for children. Alderson finds in his work a 'precarious balance between moral earnestness and levity'[18] and Whalley and Chester[19] write of his – and Leech's – 'facetiousness'. The tone of these remarks is slightly disapproving, but we should not be surprised to discover a range of shades of humour in the work of artists for whom satire and parody were normal modes of expression. More significantly, it is simply the very presence of irreverent humour that needs marking in these early attempts at forging what was then a new form.

Richard ('Dicky') Doyle was a precocious artist creating his first illustrated works by hand for the consumption of family members. He joined *Punch* at the age of nineteen in 1843 and is perhaps best known for his instantly recognisable design for the magazine's front cover. Despite the fact that he

was possessed of great facility and skill – particularly in rendering fairy-
and folk-tale matter – Doyle never became the renowned picture book
maker that the early promise suggested he might be. Alderson considers
this to be partly due to the lack of a clear market during the mid years of
the century for the kind of book that Doyle could have produced, and
partly due to a lack of confidence in, or neglect of, his ability.[20]

John Leech was the first principal *Punch* artist and the figure who,
according to Muir, made the public look at the illustrations first. With
Doyle he was the leading caricaturist in the early years of *Punch* and rarely
turned his attention to children's books, but when he did, it was clear that
he could be an illustrator of 'charm and wit' (Alderson[21]) though Whalley
and Chester[22] point to what they consider an alarming tendency towards
the grotesque. Charles Bennett was a staff artist on *Punch* too but, unlike
Leech, he seems to have diverted considerable energy into creating picture
books which he often wrote as well as illustrated following the traditional
route of trying them out on the family first. He published five books in
1848, an *Aesop's Fables, The Faithless Parrot, The Frog Who Would A-
Wooing Go, The Old Nurse's Book of Rhymes* and *Greedy Jem*. Each one is
full of lively invention and each one shows how the developing picture
book form could be varied and adapted to suit different purposes. Sadly,
Bennett died in 1867 aged 38.

Illustrators such as Crowquill, Leech, Bennett and Doyle brought to the
developing picture book a number of features that helped to shape its
future. They imported into the picture book a gaiety, liveliness and
humour that fitted the emergent form well. To the pictorial aspect of the
form they also contributed the essential formal characteristics of caricature
– simplification and exaggeration. Lastly, they began to show for the first
time how a truly *composite* text could be created from a combination of
words and pictures.

We find many of these features in the mature work of Randolph
Caldecott. Although he had no taste for exaggeration and the grotesque he
was a master of the simplification of line. Caldecott employed simplified
line drawing to create immensely expressive images, replete with narrative
significance, but his technique was far from casual. Blackburn[23] records
that he studied, 'the art of leaving out as a science; doing nothing hastily

but thinking long and seriously before putting pen to paper.' Caldecott's tongue-in-cheek maxim was, 'the fewer the lines, the less error committed.' We also find in Caldecott's work a brilliant counterpointing of words and pictures, a technique he had developed elsewhere, for example in his work for the *Graphic*. It is difficult to overestimate the importance of this feature of his work as it displayed clearly for the first time the inherent *polysemy* of picture book text, that ability the picture book has to 'thicken' and enrich the reading experience.

The simplified line and the counterpointing of word and image found its way into the picture book by another route – the comic and the cartoon strip. Picture sheets, an early ancestor of the comic strip, had been popular from the seventeenth century onwards. These were large, single-sided broadsheets with sixteen panels to a page that relied heavily upon traditional tales and well-known stories. The pictures were generally accompanied by short, verbal texts but with the work of the Swiss, Rodolphe Töpffer, there came a greater emphasis upon the role of the pictorial image. Töpffer, a teacher, is generally credited with the invention of the visual strip cartoon. In his *Album de Caricatures* published in the 1830s and 1840s the pictures tell the story while the simple one-line texts are almost superfluous. According to Gombrich[24], Töpffer discovered that the simplified pictorial language of caricature was perfectly fitted to render both *emotion* and *action*, both of which are important features of narrative. He also notes that, significantly for the picture book, it was in humorous art that the development of the knowledge of 'physiognomies' was tested out.

Töpffer's influence was felt in Britain largely through the work of the German illustrator Willhelm Busch. He was a prolific draughtsman producing many picture sheet drawings between 1849 and 1898. The illustrations to his *Schnurrdibur, oder die Bien (Buzz-a-Buzz, or the Bees* in the English edition of 1872) show clearly how the techniques exploited by Töpffer could be perfectly adapted to the animal and insect kingdoms to produce an anthropomorphism that is ingenious, witty and highly comical. Interestingly, Tenniel complained to Carroll, when preparing designs for *Through the Looking Glass*, that he was unable to illustrate an episode where Alice meets a wasp wearing a wig, 'A wasp in a wig is altogether beyond the appliances of art,' and Carroll obligingly dropped the scene. This refusal on Tenniel's part seems to indicate the limitations of his meticulously realistic style. A sparer, more linear style, oriented towards caricature could, on the evidence of Busch's *Buzz-a-Buzz*, readily have dealt with a wasp in a wig.[25]

The picture sheets and comic strips produced by illustrators such as Busch have much in common with the fully fledged comics which began to develop in the latter years of the nineteenth century. Comic strips had appeared in newspapers such as the *Graphic* from the late 1860s and *Ally Sloper's Half-Holiday* – a forerunner of the comic proper – first appeared in 1884. *Comic Cuts* and *Chips* were published in 1890 and *Funny Pips*, the first comic specially written and drawn for children, was first published in 1903. *The Gem* appeared in 1907 and *The Magnet* in 1908. By the turn of the century there was a tradition of storytelling through sequences of pictures that was already at least forty to fifty years old.

The comic continued to develop throughout the early decades of the twentieth century with more and more titles appearing on the market. The paper shortage during and after the First World War does not seem to have inhibited the growth of this particular form, its popularity and success amply bearing out Töpffer's belief that caricature storytelling appeals powerfully to the general population as well as to children. The comic also proved to be fertile ground for experimentation, both in the kinds of stories that could be portrayed in pictures and in the formal means by which the stories could be realised.

However, the comic and the comic strip began to have an influence upon the development of picture books only in the middle years of the twentieth century when illustrators, like Edward Ardizzone, began to appreciate the narrative potential of comic strip techniques and when the comic itself began to achieve a modicum of respectability with the gradual acceptance by the book-reading public of strips such as Hergé's *Tintin* and Goscinny and Uderzo's *Asterix*.

Eventually picture book makers of skill and flair began to deploy for their own ends the full range of techniques developed within the comic strip form. Maurice Sendak in America and Raymond Briggs and Shirley Hughes in the UK, for example, have at various times since the sixties shown how the comic strip can be used to powerful and varied effect. Briggs has perhaps explored more thoroughly than anyone else the emotional and dramatic range of the comic strip, transforming the picture sequence into a flexible narrative form. He has demonstrated this flexibility and range in books as different in temper and tones as *Father Christmas, Fungus the Bogeyman, The Snowman, Gentleman Jim, When the Wind Blows, The Tin-Pot Foreign General and the Old Iron Woman* and *Unlucky Wally*. More recently he has embedded picture sequences into much longer, complex narratives such as *The Man*.

The contemporary picture book would not be in the form we now recognise were it not for the influence of the nineteenth-century caricaturists and the resolutely populist makers of comics and comic strips. They have not only added to the extraordinary flexibility of the form but have ensured that it possesses humour and irony, narrative drive and power and, perhaps most importantly, a complexity and richness born of the counterpointing of words and pictures.

When we look back to the origins of the picture book and to its development through the nineteenth century I believe we can detect a number of important features that have survived to the present day and which give the picture book its unique character. There is its brevity, and its interweaving of word and image, both originally inherited from the chapbook. These are the features that give the form its flexibility, its willingness to ingest other genres and forms of representation, and its ability to hybridise – sometimes bizarrely – with games and toys. This lack of respect for genre boundaries and conventions goes hand in hand with a general air of irreverence born equally of the picture book's folkloric origins and of the shaping experience it had in the hands of the nineteenth century caricaturists. This latter body of artists and writers not only injected wit and humour and narrative energy into the form, they introduced a degree of irony by exploiting and thereby demonstrating its capacity for counterpointing word and image. More than anything else the history of the picture book shows clearly that the form is inherently heterogeneous, not so much a genre itself but a uniquely flexible, composite kind of text more than capable of adapting itself to changes in the wider culture.

REFERENCES

1 Brian Alderson, *Sing a Song for Sixpence: the English Picture Book Tradition and Randolph Caldecott.* Cambridge: Cambridge University Press in association with the British Library 1986.

2 J. I. Whalley and T. R. Chester. *A History of Children's Book Illustration.* London: John Murray with the Victoria and Albert Museum, 1988 p. 216.

3 ibid. pp. 216–17.

4 Alderson, op. cit.

5 Percy Muir, *English Children's Books, 1600–1900.* London: Batsford, 1954, footnote to p. 67.

6 R. M. Slythe, *The Art of Illustration 1750–1900.* London: The Library Association, 1970, p. 13.

7 Elaine Moss, *W(h)ither Picture Books: Some Tricks of the Trade, Signal 31.* Stroud: Thimble Press, 1980.

8 F. J. Harvey Darton, *Children's Books in England: Five Centuries of Social Life.* Cambridge: Cambridge University Press, 3rd edition, 1982, p. 69.

9 Robert Leeson, *Reading and Righting.* London: Collins, 1985, p. 59.

10 William Feaver, *When We Were Young: Two Centuries of Children's Book Illustration.* London: Thames and Hudson, 1977, p. 9.

11 J. H. Plumb, essay in G. Gottlieb (ed.), *Early Children's Books and their Illustration.* London: the Pierpont Morgan Library and Oxford University Press, 1975.

12 Muir, 1954, op. cit., p. 210.

13 J. A. Smith, *Children's Illustrated Books.* London: Collins, 1948.

14 Muir, 1954, op. cit.

15 Maurice Sendak, *Caldecott and Co.: Notes on Books and Pictures.* London: Reinhardt Books in association with Viking, 1988.

16 Muir, op. cit.

17 Feaver, op. cit.

18 Alderson, op. cit. p. 65.

19 Whalley and Chester, op. cit. p. 56.

20 Alderson, op. cit.

21 Alderson, op. cit., p. 71.

22 Whalley and Chester, op. cit.

23 H. Blackburn, *Randolph Caldecott: A Personal Memoir of his Early Art Career.* London: Sampson Low, Marston, Searle and Rivington, 1886, p. 126.

21

24 E. Gombrich, *Art and Illusion: A Study in the Psychology of Pictorial Representation.* London: Phaidon Press, 1960.

25 See E. Hodnett, *Image and Text: Studies in the Illustration of English Literature.* London: Scolar Press, 1982.

2

Inside the tunnel: a radical kind of reading – picture books, pupils and post-modernism

Morag Styles

There are three central ideas behind this chapter: the first is that young children are intellectually engaged with picture books and have a great deal to teach adults about them; the second is that many picture books are extraordinarily interesting and complicated texts which demand sophisticated reading; and the third, is a speculation about whether one of the attractions of young readers to these texts is the complex, game-playing stance of post-modernism. She goes on to argue that many artists are working in a post-modernist mode which often involves a kind of humour which has a great deal in common with children's play. This is why children are drawn to it and find it easy to comprehend: it works with the grain of childhood. Morag Styles' respect for picture books is clear, but it is the insightful voices of young readers which come across most strongly in this chapter.

❛ You seem, as the artist-narrator, almost to have destroyed the formal, predictable patterns and created new ones . . . ❜

Charlotte Otten to Maurice Sendak[1]

❛ . . . . the picture book, which appears to be the cosiest and most gentle of genres, actually produces the greatest social and aesthetic tensions in the whole field of children's literature. ❜

Sheila Egoff[2]

If the picture book produced 'the greatest social and aesthetic tensions in the whole field of children's literature' in 1981, how much more are Sheila Egoff's words true in the 1990s. Margaret Meek calls them 'a site for radical experimentation . . . [with their] artistic and iconic intrigue, imaginative verve . . . and inventive formats'.[3] But, exciting picture books are not a late twentieth-century phenomenon. I do not simply mean that there were artists from the eighteenth century to the present day whose originality and talent were devoted to illustrating books for children: from Thomas Bewick, born in 1753, to Kate Greenaway who died in 1901; not to mention fine nineteenth-century illustrators such as Richard Doyle, Arthur Rackham, the Robinson brothers, Arthur Hughes, Ernest Shepard (who straddles this century, of course) and others. What I want to stress is that gifted artists have always gone well beyond aesthetically pleasing embellishments of text. And the hallmark of illustrators as diverse as Beatrix Potter, Randolph Caldecott, Walter Crane, N. C. Wyeth and, earlier this century, Edward Ardizzone, is their ability to add new dimensions to the printed text by playing with it, subverting it, questioning it, being suggestive with it, or turning it upside down. These artists went beyond the conventions of their time; their illustrations added layers of meaning to the written word. Maurice Sendak has been a distinguished exponent of this art since 1952 and his comments show how this complexity and playfulness is intentional and carefully crafted.

‹ To be an illustrator is to be . . . someone who has something just as important to say as the writer of the book – occasionally something even more important . . . I'm interested in . . . interpretative illustration . . . You must leave a space in the text so the picture can do the work . . . the illustrator is doing a tremendous job of expansion, of collaboration, of illumination . . . A picture book has to have that incredible seamless look to it when it's finished. One stitch showing and you've lost the game . . . The peculiar gift in being an illustrator is that one has an odd affinity with words, that it's natural to interpret words, almost like a composer think-ing music when reading poetry.[4]   ›

If picture books are more complex than many commentators realise, if they offer interest to adults as well as children, if many of the illustrators who create them have complicated intentions, what, you may ask, has that got to do with the current debate on the teaching of reading? (When has there not been a debate on the teaching of reading?) One of its central concerns is the nature of the texts with which children learn to read; as the spurious argument goes – 'real books' versus reading schemes. This is not the moment to unpick the fallacy of this crude dichotomy within which many commentators on the reading debate, who should know better, seem to operate. (See Waterland: 1989: Styles 1994 for a summary.)[5] But it is worth reminding ourselves that 'real books' are, by and large, picture books. For some teachers, it is the sheer quality of these texts as literature which makes them so convinced that children must have the best possible reading material from the start. Here is David Lewis talking about a popular picture book:

> ‹ If we are willing to heed its lessons then I think that *Where's Julius?* can teach us a great deal about children's books and about the nature of reading. Furthermore, if the kind of literacy we wish for our children is a critical literacy, if we wish them to have some kind of understanding of how different forms of writing work – and work upon them, as readers – then we could do far worse than to explore effective and appropriate ways of using books like *Where's Julius?* with beginning readers.[6] ›

There is also the uncontroversial fact that many picture books do a rather good job for inexperienced readers in providing texts and pictures which are not only inviting, but actually support the early stages of reading. (See, for example, Meek, 1988, on *Rosie's Walk*; Graham, 1990 on *Granpa*; Watson, 1994 on *The Tunnel*.) [7]

Margaret Meek has shown us how some pictorial texts actually teach young readers sophisticated lessons about how narrative works: that the story is made up of words and pictures together; that what is not said can be the most significant element in the story; that reading is a game with lots of different rules; that there are cultural features in all children's stories; that patterns are created with an infinite number of variations; that when we want to make new meanings we often use metaphor; that words mean more than they say; that different kinds of storytelling can exist side by side, each having different conventions; that written discourse is infinitely various.[8]

Influenced by Meek and others, junior and secondary school teachers are now examining the value of pictorial texts with older pupils. (Many teachers of early years and some children's librarians and booksellers were way ahead – they had been trying to tell the rest of us for years that we

25

needed to take picture books more seriously.) Unsurprisingly, teachers of older pupils have found that more experienced readers take great pleasure in reading and analysing these texts and, indeed, constructing their own. Artists like Anthony Browne, Maurice Sendak, John Burningham, Raymond Briggs come into their own, as their books deal with issues as challenging as: divorce and remarriage (*The Visitors Who Came To Stay*, Browne, 1987); gender (*Piggybook*, Browne, 1986); adults' neglect of children/the child's sense of responsibility (*Outside Over There*, Sendak, 1981); isolation and bullying (*Aldo*, Burningham, 1991); death (*Granpa*, Burningham, 1984); difference, disability, prejudice (*The Man*, Briggs, 1994); love and loss (*The Snowman*, Briggs, 1985); nuclear war (*When The Wind Blows*, Briggs, 1982) to name but a few. Peter Hunt agrees with me on Briggs:

❦ 'Another illustrator whose preoccupations have enabled him to work across the age range is Raymond Briggs . . . His pessimistic and brutal realism within the context of the cosy-looking cartoon strip developed from the sad fatalism of *Gentleman Jim* (1980) to the apocalyptic and merciless *When The Wind Blows.* (1982)[9] ❧

Artists like these often use humour to soften some of the potential harshness of their themes. But it is not only older children who enjoy picture books with challenging themes and big ideas. This, and the humour, is what many children as young as five find so gripping. Recently I have been reading picture books with five-and six-year-olds in my local school. About twenty of my favourite picture books are spread out on a large table and a small group of children are allowed to select what they want to read. (My range includes all the artists listed above, plus the Ahlbergs, Ruth Brown, Shirley Hughes, Satoshi Kitamura, David McKee, Jan Ormerod, Jan Pienkowski, Posy Simmonds and Smith and Scieszka.) It wasn't just the younger children who responded to my collection of picture books, as if they had entered Aladdin's cave; older pupils walking past us gazed longingly at the books, begged to be allowed to read them or ventured comments about some 'really brill' titles. As for my own little group, while appreciating all the authors, they overwhelmingly went for Anthony Browne. Pictures that often confused or intrigued me were pored over by little people, laughing aloud, eagerly devouring every visual joke. Inevitably, they noticed things I didn't, even when it was a book I thought I had examined closely. I soon realised that these children, particularly those who could not yet read print, were excited by two particular features of these texts – their humour and their profundity.

Justin and Wong Lee, aged six and five respectively, chose to read Anthony Browne's *Zoo*.[10] There were books on offer that were funnier, easier and more light-hearted, but they were quite clear it was this challenging text that they wanted to explore. The boys were soon deeply engaged in unravelling the many perplexing motifs in Browne's work: unworried by surrealist imagery, visual puns or enigmatic representation, they scrutinised the text with great determination to find every possible incongruity, laughing with delight whenever they did so. Justin and Wong Lee were also reading Browne for his serious concerns. Here are some notes I took of their spoken comments on my first visit.

■ The cover's like a zebra . . .
The giraffes look a bit happier . . . look, it's a bit lighter . . .
All those people are . . . (they identify various animals) . . . they're a bit like the animals at the zoo . . .
They've been cheeky monkeys (referring to the boys wearing monkey masks)
It's like a puzzle . . .
He's all alone . . . he's got no friends . . . it's too dark . . . like the night-time . . . he's sad because he looks like he's behind bars . . . (on the final spread). ■

Of course, young children can't articulate the nature of their intellectual absorption. When I asked them why they liked the book, Justin said it was funny and Wong Lee said he enjoyed it 'because it's a monster kind of thing!' I am willing to bet that both these children had a strong sense of Browne's own condemnation of animals kept in captivity, saw the parallels and irony between the brutish (animal-like?) way that human beings sometimes behave and the dignity of the animals, and empathised with the boy's shame and discomfort at the end of the story. I have no hard evidence for this, except the tape-recording of our conversation and my recollection of how they pointed eagerly at images, exclaimed aloud, laughed, and looked puzzled; the number of times they went back to look at pictures, compared one with another; and their quick throw-away comments that suggested that this adult was a bit daft to ask them such obvious things.

In fact, their discourse was full of shared understandings that didn't need to be spoken, and only required acknowledgement by a brief word, nod or smile. When Justin said, 'Anthony Browne's books are funny', Wong Lee nodded fiercely in agreement. I know that the word 'funny' carried reference to a huge range of humorous devices they appreciated in Browne's work. On my second visit I brought in the then newly published *The Big Baby*. 'It's by Anthony Browne,' said Justin excitedly. I asked him how he knew, wondering if he could read Browne's name. 'Because I know the pictures he does!' Justin's surprise at the teacher's stupid question showed his competence at reading artistic style.

The boys are learning that picture books tackle powerful issues and probe difficult areas of life in a way that the rest of the curriculum cannot do. Small children can't yet handle demanding discussions, can't read much printed text and can't yet express themselves in writing, except very simply, unless, for the latter, adults act as scribes. They can *draw* complicated narratives, but that's another story to pursue another time. At this point I would simply draw the reader's attention to a possible link between the complexity of children's drawing and their interest in the pictures in picture books, the productive and receptive modes of visual literacy.

Looking at a couple of drawings by my six-year-old nephew, Tom, illustrates my argument. In the first picture (figure 2) 'Warrior' is dressed in lavish, shining, intricately patterned armour. Every stud, buckle and joint is embellished in silver which also adorns his red gauntlets and gun. The title is in silver, the border around the drawing is in silver; so are his eyes and the extra guns he wears by his side, for he brandishes a sword in one hand and a rifle in the other. The sky is a serene blue and the sun a brilliant yellow; both these colours are echoed on the warrior's person. There is so much that could be analysed in this dramatic little drawing, one of about twenty that Tom dashes off daily. I will just mention three things. The first is that every aspect of that drawing is thought about and has a purpose; there is more than spontaneity about this carefully crafted warrior. The second is that this peace-loving six-year-old delights in the

Figure 2 'Warrior' by Tom, aged six

accoutrements of war and heroes, happily mixing genres and taking from toys, television and books that have been read to him. I don't believe this fascination will do him any harm; if you are small in a big, uncertain, adult world, perhaps you need to create powerful warriors to support you and to help you imagine that one day you might be big and strong too. Finally, I want to emphasise the detailed knowledge that went into the drawing, let alone the complex ideas that lay behind it.

The second drawing (figure 3) is of a man shooting a bird. I invited Tom to tell me what was going on, and here is Tom's own (reluctant!) explanation. Remember that only a fraction of the thinking that has gone into this five minute work of art can be articulated.

■ Mighty Max is against a bad bird. He's shooting it with a pistol. He's smiling because he's shot the bird. He's wearing a cap. He's standing on a heat-line, but it won't get him as he's got special shoes on. He's got like sonic-shoes with all different colours and leather trousers. That end bit of the heat-line goes slow. When the bird falls on it, he will be a fossil. ■

29

Figure 3 **'Mighty Max' by Tom, aged six**

School learning mixed with popular media texts. Yet none of it conveys the drama of his composition – the cool, elegantly clad superhero with the cap trendily positioned the wrong way round, smiling confidently at the viewer; the way the carefully chosen colours reflect the mood; the clever techniques borrowed from comics to convey the action. Drawings are a vehicle for expressing developing intellects at work as well as artistic skill.

So, picture books offer children access to the serious issues of life in an accessible form and with humour. No wonder children love them. Margaret Meek suggests that the difficulty in reading for many children 'lies not in the words but in understanding something that lies behind the words, embedded in the sense . . . so that the text means more than it says.'[11] Quality picture books teach these intricate lessons and children seem hungry for such rich nourishment. As with any diet, though, they also need a bit of junk and things that slide down easily, now and again.

Going back to my school visit, Rashid, aged six, taught me another important lesson about reading picture books. After we had explored Jan

Pienkowski's *Haunted House*[12] together, opening every flap, turning every dial, pulling every arrow, Rashid asked me firmly to read it again. As we had spent a long time on the book already, I groaned inwardly, keen to get more data on children responding to picture books. As Rashid had just looked intently, making very few comments, it was difficult to assess her response to the text. However, off we went on another reading, trying out all the pop-up technology again. When we had completed it a second time, she requested a further reading. I knew it was important to her, because of her serious expression and because she was unmistakably engrossed, so I felt obliged to go through *Haunted House* one final time. Rashid was satisfied at last and I realised something glaringly obvious about pictorial texts. It took Rashid three 'lookings' to get a sense of the book. Why hadn't I understood this simple fact before? It takes longer to absorb pictures than it does print and, as Rashid didn't yet have access to print, her only reading was the pictorial text which she studied as thoroughly as any scholar. *Haunted House* is a delightful, playful and amusing text; it isn't serious in itself, but Rashid's desire to have a complete experience of it was nothing short of single-minded.

My next visit to school confirmed my hunches about children's ability to interpret and negotiate complex pictorial texts. This time I was reading *The Frog Prince Continued* by Steve Johnson and Jon Scieszka[13] with Kate, a fluent reader aged six, and Justin, also six, who was just beginning to manage printed text. After reading the section on the first spread where it says that the prince and princess were unhappy together, I asked the children if there was anything in the picture that suggested they were not happy.

■ **Kate**   He is sticking his tongue out (*it looked like a frog's tongue*) and the tulips are weeping. And there's a frog on the chair . . .

Justin   Because the prince was actually a frog . . .

Kate   Yes, with two frog eyes and frog legs . . . (*referring to the chair*)

M.S.   Is there anything in the picture to say that he's getting more frog-like?

Kate   Yes, he's jumping in the mirror and he's wearing green.

Justin   I know — the pillow is like a lily-pad, (*we had already spotted these on the endpapers*) . . . and there's weeds . . .

Kate   And him looking nervous . . . and the colours . . .

Justin   Green, green, all green. His cover is green and his bedroom is green.   ■

Later we encountered a variety of witches in strange settings, one of whom asks the prince if he is looking for a sleeping princess to wake up.

Kate Because that's the story of the sleeping beauty . . .

Justin And that says the fairest . . . he's in the wrong story . . .

M.S. What story is that?

Justin Snow White And The Seven Dwarfs.

Kate I know – Hansel and Gretel, the sweet house . . .

Justin Lollipops.

Kate No they're M & Ms . . . and I know who that is. It's the fairy god-mother in Cinderella.

Justin Look it's turning pumpkins into carriages.

Kate It's going to have to turn back. . . . I know because I've read Cinderella.

Despite the huge differential in their ability to read print, both these children were equally capable 'multilayered readers', effortlessly making intertextual links. As Peter Hunt[14] points out:

‘ One of the paradoxes of children's reading is that a verbal text, while it may have immense interactive potential, may also disguise by virtue of the inexperience of the reader . . . Picture books have a more immediate effect; they are more accessible, they literally show as well as tell. ’

In a recent article, David Lewis[15] argues that many picture books are post-modernist and appeal to children because of the playful nature of such texts. One of the reasons children find them so entertaining is because they haven't yet got stuck on the traditional rules of the game and anyway they like to play.

‘ . . . many of the picture books we offer to young children . . . work against the realist grain and offer, for readers of all ages, the opportunity for a playful exploration of what is involved in the making and interpretation of literary fictions. . . . Post-modernism . . . is a rule-breaking kind of art for it achieves its effects precisely by parodying and calling into question those very rules and conventions upon which the more traditional forms of narrative fiction depend . . . ’

Lewis suggests that in the work of contemporary picture book makers there is 'a willingness to break boundaries, subvert conventions and parody the settled norms of storytelling . . . where the stability, order and decorum of the realist text [is] regularly transgressed.'

I wish to examine Lewis's thesis about post-modernism and the picture book and to consider whether it is the 'rule-breaking' nature of many picture books which gives them such appeal to children. What is it about picture books that makes them a good vehicle for revealing capacities and competences in children that many adults did not suspect they had? Before looking more closely at the theory and the books, it needs to be underlined that our thinking has moved beyond what Geoff Moss[16] describes as:

> ‘ the form of writing generally exemplified in fiction for children [which] invites the reader to accept that the author has expressed his or her personality in a unique vision or interpretation of the world and the reader has direct access to that personality. Technique and structure are backgrounded so that the message of the text is conveyed through an apparently neutral or transparent medium which allows the utmost identification with the author's intention.　　　　　　　　　’

Critical theory has opened our eyes to what now seems a naive view of literature, whatever critical position we adopt. Do the books that David Lewis[17] describes as 'designed and marketed for those readers at the very beginning of their journey into literacy' refuse to take for granted the settled and time-honoured norms of how stories should be told and written?

Picture books as metafictive texts

> ‘ In many of our favourite picture books the conventions are there for all to see . . . In their artful and playful juxtaposition of image and word they often seek to draw attention to the fabric of the text itself.'
>
> **David Lewis**[18] ’

> ‘ . . . metafiction . . . denies that language is invisible and prevents total absorption or identification with a book . . . By highlighting, and drawing attention to the conventions or means of production within the text,

such devices produce readers who are both capable of emotional involvement in a text and aware of how that text has been constructed. **,**

Geoff Moss[19]

Because of the metafictive nature of many picture books, how the texts are constructed and by whom are questions which can be explained to many young readers. Smith and Scieszka are particularly good at this. Look, for example, at *The Stinky Cheese Man and other fairly stupid tales* or *The True Story Of The Three Little Pigs.*[20] In the former, the authors query all sorts of aspects of book construction from who the author is, to what the ISBN number signifies; from the use of different sorts of font for effect, to the nature of the contents page. You can't read *The Stinky Cheese Man* without engaging with these bibliographic details, let alone considering the nature of narrative, authorial voice and intertextuality, though most young readers will not have access to these terms. Similarly, in *The True Story Of The Three Little Pigs,* the sepia colours of old newspaper print and photography, the central character's insistence that he is telling the *true* story of the big bad wolf, the journalistic style (not to say old Hollywood movies and a Philip Marlowesque voice) insists on a dialogue between reader and author on versions of 'the truth'. Jane Doonan [21] puts it better:

' . . . the art of irony by word and picture, the delights of parody, the rhythms and vocabulary of oral storytelling, the various and distinctive forms of fictional and factional and factual writing . . . the position of an outsider within a society . . . The story is by Alexander T. Wolf, but since he is being held in the pig penitentiary, he has to use the services of a ghost writer . . . Along with a text which talks the telling are two conflicting newspaper accounts of the events. The lead story in THE DAILY WOLF is illustrated by a large photograph of a distinguished, bespectacled gentlewolf in a white shirt, bow tie, pinstriped jacket . . . THE DAILY PIG, however, displays a shot of a mean, lean, black silhouette huffing and puffing beneath the banner headline BIG BAD WOLF . . . As well as making an observation on the nature of their value of what is printed in newspapers, Lane Smith's way of picturing carries visual reference to the use of the printed word in pictures with its historical chain from the Cubists through to . . . artists who graft together various types of representational language. **,**

Picture books and complexity

‘ Of course, the real purpose of any great story – whether for children or
for adults – is to create many levels . . . a book without these qualities, in
my opinion, is not worth a second reading. . . .   ’

Otten[22]

Many picture books today are extremely complex in all sorts of ways. It
might be that the pictures tell a story at variance with the printed text, as
in *Rosie's Walk*; or the author is playing with two different story lines at
the same time, as in Burningham's *Come away from the water, Shirley*.
Kitamura depicts a set of comic-frightening scenarios, but only for *one* of
the characters in *Lily Takes A Walk*. Lily herself has a perfectly ordinary
stroll down the street. Which is the 'real' story? Sometimes the narrative is
difficult to follow, as in McKee's *I Hate My Teddy Bear* or *Not Now,
Bernard*. I'm still unsure what the former is about, but it certainly is fun
trying to work it out. Peter Hunt[23] has the same problem:

‘ David McKee's masterpiece is probably *I Hate My Teddy Bear* . . .
McKee's art is deceptive; he challenges the very way in which we organ-
ise our concepts of reality, as compared with a child. By flattening out
the whole complex landscapes he deals with the way in which the child
sees all parts of the world as equal. Perspective has to be learned.   ’

These books offer pluralities of possibilities, different voices, more than
one version of a story which make demands on the reader to struggle with
the meaning rather than presenting a straightforward story. Children are
often good at this sort of reading which in many ways mirrors their 'play'.
Anthony Browne[24] is explicit about making the reader work hard in his
description of Hansel and Gretel.

‘ I decided I didn't want to do a pretty book, because it's not a pretty story
. . . it was a story of poverty. I decided that there were going to be
certain themes in the book – and one of them is of prison, of cages, of
bars . . . I wanted to introduce into the story the idea of transformation
. . . I wanted to suggest that the stepmother, in the eyes of the children
at least, is the same person as the witch . . . and (at the end) there's a
new shoot growing out of the plant pot and Arnold Bocklin's *Isle of the*

> *Dead* on the windowsill . . . I often use paintings on the wall to try and tell another aspect of the story. . . .   ›

Browne believes that young readers can handle complexity; at the same time he demonstrates his, probably unconscious, fascination with the playful, rule-breaking stance of post-modernism.

Picture books and fragmentation

‹ Much post-structuralist theory . . . tries to disrupt a human-centred view of the world and argues that the subject is constructed in language and discourse – and split, unstable and fragmented . . . the picture book is a series of frames, materially marked by borders or page edges, and the portrayal of character or landscape is necessarily fragmented . . .   ›

Geoff Moss[25]

Geoff Moss suggests that picture books are, of their very nature, fragmented. Certainly, small children quickly learn to cope with a bewildering array of formats from the simple picture on one side of a spread with text below or opposite, to the wide range of 'strips' employed by Posy Simmonds in *Lulu* and *The Chocolate Wedding* or Shirley Hughes in *Up And Up* (both are discussed elsewhere in this book). *Angry Arthur* is, I suppose, the most obvious example of fragmentation as it shows the disintegrating force of anger: Arthur's rage threatens the stability of the very universe in Kitamura's powerful and jarring illustrations. And you never know in Scieszka's *The Stinky Cheese Man* what the Little Red Hen will do or say next, what story she will move into or change, how she will disorder the typeface or the index, or challenge any of the conventions we take for granted about how books work.

Picture books and playfulness

Picture books are arguably the richest area of experimentation in children's literature at the moment. The possibilities of what can be done with a picture book take us to the limits of paper engineering (*The Jolly Christmas Postman*, for example, is a miracle of inventiveness), make intertextual reference to the entire history of art and literature, open up the way different cultures operate and the role of the dominant culture within society, deals with all the great issues of life, except, perhaps, close attention to sex and violence, though they are by no means excluded. T. S. Eliot begins to look quite a straight-forward writer! And it is all achieved through playful means or the attention of young readers would be quickly lost. Here's Anthony Browne[26] describing how he went about the illustration for Alice falling down the rabbit hole. The playfulness of the original written text is echoed by the artist's creativity.

‘ . . . I drew the shelves – but I didn't know what was going to be on them. As I actually painted the picture I started off at the top and meandered down, almost putting in anything that came into my head but that had relevance to the story – even though it may have been an illogical relevance – a bit like a dream. So as she is falling down, she is wondering about what it would be like to come out in Australia where people walk upside down. So I did a little blackboard, as if she may be dreaming about her geography lessons at school, with a picture of Australia – upside down. There are things that vaguely relate to the story – keys, teapot, pig. For instance, she is thinking about her per cat, Dinah, as she is falling down again and she wonders if cats eat bats. So I showed a pet cat's bowl with Dinah written on and a cricket bat in it. She is trying to remember her geography lessons, and I used a map that was drawn by the surrealists . . . so England doesn't actually exist. ’

David Lewis[27] outlines some of the enigmatic qualities in *Where's Julius?* using his own children's reactions to the book.

‘ The pictures in *Where's Julius?* then seem to fall into two broad categories: those that accompany the domestic scenes and those that atmospherically and powerfully depict the sites of Julius's wanderings. The former tend to be, like the written text, rather similar in outline and not especially memorable. The latter are large and bold and are clearly designed for uninterrupted contemplation. . . . Simon and Claire seemed not at all perturbed by the switch from recognisable and familiar domestic play to an altogether more indeterminate realm of the fantastic. It is, however, important that we ask, and seek to answer, the question of just where Julius is at the very moment when we are closest to seeing what is going on. For there is a strong invitation within the text to perceive events as all belonging to the same generic category, that of consistent realism. Our urge to naturalise the tale, to normalise it in this way, is encouraged by an author/illustrator intent upon subverting the very expectations he arouses. '

Picture books and incompleteness

' Post-modernism pictures a subjective, relativistic world which is so full of contradiction and so dependent on individual observers for its definition that there is little certainty about anything. . . . '

Geoff Moss[28]

' You make it up 'cos then it sounds exciting when you make stuff up. Lucy, aged 6[29] '

All wordless picture books fall into the category of 'incompleteness', as the reader has to supply the written text for herself. In an unguarded moment, I asked a student to remind me of the boy's name in Raymond Briggs' wordless text, *The Snowman*. It is such a deep and vivid text that I momentarily forgot that I had supplied some of its detailed richness myself. When Lynda Teichler was studying some of her five- and six-year-olds' responses to Shirley Hughes's outstanding wordless picture book, *Up and Up*, she noticed how they were questioning the visual text all the time, making hypotheses about why various things were happening, supplying what was missing from the visual narrative or filling in the gaps. Here are some extracts from her transcript which show the children (Holly age four, Ashley and Alison age five, and Lucy and Ryan age six) at work.

On the opening page Holly suggested, 'She's thinking about if she can fly', but was corrected by Ashley, who said, 'She's thinking she <u>wants</u> to fly.' Later on the same page: 'She's very dizzy,' ventured Holly. 'I've seen that on Roger Rabbit,' remarked Ryan. When Lynda Teichler asked the children why the picture was in black and white, Lucy volunteered that 'probably it's an old story'. Lucy then noticed the old-fashioned clock on page 6: 'It's her grandad's because mums and dads don't have that kind of clock – they have a circle one.'

Figure 4 From *Up and Up* by Shirley Hughes, published by Bodley Head

On page 9, the bus queue watch the central character fly through the air

■ **Lucy**	They're thinking – well that's strange. Any other girl can't fly.
Ryan	Amazing. Watch where you're going, will you!
Lucy	(*mimicking an adult voice*) Watch where you're going, young lady!
Teacher	(*looking at page 10*) What sort of man do you think he is? (*Hughes has drawn a stereotype of a male scientist.*)
Lucy	An experimentalist.
Holly	An old man.
Ryan	A scientist, he looks like she's getting on his nerves.
Teacher	(*looking at page 22*) What do you think she is saying?
Ryan	(*blowing a raspberry*) Come and get me!
Lucy	I hate you.
Teacher	(*looking at page 27*) Why are they shaking hands?
Ryan	She's saying she's sorry.
Lucy	They was silly to each other first but now they're making up friends.
Alison	To so 'cos she's very well . . . so, cos she, 'cos the man's shaking her hand to be . . . to be very well trying. ■

And if you look at the illustration (figure 5), you'll see just what Alison meant! Finally, on page 28 when the central character looks up at the

Figure 5 **From *Up and Up* by Shirley Hughes, published by Bodley Head**

bird, Lucy commented, 'She thinks "Oh no I won't try that again".' Very wise.

Picture books and the ability to shock

Picture books regularly violate our common sense view of the world through visual nonsense and perceptual incongruities. As Anthony Browne makes clear in *A Walk In The Park*[30]:

‘ I try to pretend that the details in the background were consciously try-ing to reflect the imagination of the child – that the parents were very cold and dogmatic and dressed in their armour . . . but the children take off their overcoats . . . and copy the dogs and play together as the dogs do without any barrier between them. So I am trying to suggest that Robin Hood, and the tree that becomes a foot, and the man walking the tomato . . . were a conscious decision on my part to reflect the children's minds. But I don't actually think they were. I think in those days I just included these things in the background, partly to interest me and partly because I felt insecure about the simple nature of the story. ’

In Sendak's latest book, *We Are All In The Dumps with Jack And Guy*[31], he gives two traditional nursery rhymes a post-modernist treatment by setting them in a homeless community of children (and cats), some with shaved heads, others with what Jane Doonan suggests are echoes of the tough-guy Artful Dodger and Oliver Twist. After a brief glance, you know you are looking at a masterpiece. There is a towering humanity of vision, anger at injustice, compassion for the weak. Reading this book you cannot escape the issues of poverty and homelessness and greed. Jane Doonan[32] says.

‹ The Dumps kids are placed in a deprived setting. They are barefoot, barely clad in hand-me-downs or newspapers, and some little bald heads suggest they know about treatment for cancers. The newsprint either records death and disasters – AIDS, world famine, chaos in shelters, shootings, redundancies – or is ironic in the extreme, announcing mortgages, investment opportunities, housing schemes, bank booms. The architectural style of the bakery, with its grey walls, barred windows and tall chimney, and the tiered rows of bunks within the bleak interior, calls to mind descriptions of concentration camps.   ›

But Sendak's children are never entirely victims: they are brave, resourceful and cunning, as he knows children to be.

The first of many shocks in *We Are All In The Dumps* is the front cover with no title or author. These details are on the back. It commands us to pay attention to what is being depicted on the front cover, rather than to focus on conventions like who wrote or published the book. Perhaps the omission of the expected cover features are a metaphor for what is missing from the nameless, unknown poor and deprived of the world who enjoy few human rights. (I am indebted to Victor Watson for this insight.) Lucy Pyatt[33] suggests

‹ Sendak breaks all the usual conventions, but he gives us some clues as to the content. He lines up the figures as though they were on stage. He clothes the homeless children in newspapers with headlines hinting at what is to come (*Leaner Times/Meaner Times*). He alludes to the flipside of poverty with ironic messages of 'very smart living' and 'mortgage money available' . . . The whiteness of the moon, whilst also framing the characters, contrasts starkly with the saturated red of the sky and the blackness of the hole.   ›

Some of the newspaper headlines were more encouraging: 'Kid Elected President' and 'Children Triumph'. Is Sendak suggesting that children might be better at solving some of the world's problems than the adults who currently hold positions of power? Certainly, he makes the reader question basic values and morality and, indeed, the competence and decency of political leaders. I felt moved, excited, angry and inspired when I first read *We Are All In The Dumps*. Several readings on, I have traced various pictorial metaphors through the text, 'read' the complex role of colour in the book, examined the issues of power, poverty, corruption, illness and greed and am still puzzling over countless meanings I cannot decipher. I know that when I read this book twenty years on, there will still be more for me to discover.

I recently showed *We Are All In The Dumps* to a group of primary teachers, and the overwhelming reaction was, indeed, shock, and in many cases, disapproval, that a book so full of painful and worrying images and ideas could be suitable for children. I find this point of view bemusing, as I have never known a child to look closely at a book he or she finds disagreeable. Children are their own censors. Sometimes they approach books with a mixture of fear and desire and the attraction may be stronger than the repulsion. At other times, they are unequivocal. Here is Rashid again (remember, she loved the creepy *Haunted House*). She has just rejected Browne's *Bear Goes To Town*[34] with a shudder of distaste at an illustration of a gruesome butcher's shop: 'I don't like it. We are vegetarian. I don't like to see sausage'. Rashid wasn't only disgusted at Browne's depiction of 'sausage' – there were also different kinds of meat clearly related to the animals from which they came, a pool of blood, some dismembered heads of pigs . . . She was probably also reacting to the hint of menace which pervades the book and to images that clashed with her sense of propriety and cultural expectations. Rashid was perfectly clear that after a quick look at this book, she didn't want to read it. Children must be allowed to exercise this choice and preference, but surely teachers must also be allowed to include on the library shelves books they think are challenging and well constructed, even if some will have minority appeal.

I suspect that the hostile reaction by some to *We Are All In The Dumps* is the 90s version of the furore which greeted publication of *Where The Wild Things Are* in the 60s, a book which is now widely considered to be a 'classic'. The problem is for adults and their sensibilities, rather than the children. We can trace adults' determination to control and censor books for children back through history and always in the name of concern for the young. Why shouldn't small children engage in some of the harsher realities of life if they want to? Sendak presents the issues in a way that is accessible to children, if they are ready for it, larded with light relief, visual fun and through the vehicle of an old rhyme. Lucy Pyatt found that the children she consulted 'recounted their own experiences and reflected their knowledge of situations such as loneliness, upset and bullying. "The moon bullied Jack and Guy so they wouldn't bully the poor little kid," said a ten year old. Another stated, "We should talk about homelessness."[35] A lot of the children, especially the younger ones, paid a great deal of attention to the kittens in the story.' When a book works on many levels, as this one does, less experienced readers take what they are able from the text. And if children do understand the themes that are being explored, the reality is shocking – the reader should be shocked.

Summary

Anthony Browne's *The Tunnel*[36] gave me the title for this chapter and this is the text with which I wish to close this discussion, as it draws on various features of post-modernism and shows how one book can tap into so many veins. First of all, it is an incomplete text in that there are illustrations which simply don't make sense unless the reader puts the different elements of the jigsaw together. Victor Watson[37] shows how a child as young as four was able to make an insightful closure of an open text for herself.

‘ Ann had been in her reception class about a month when she chose to read with me a book she had not seen before (*The Tunnel*) . . . She noticed that in a corner of the final endpaper the boy's football and the girl's story-book are side by side. I showed her that the opening endpaper was identical *except that there was no football* and asked her why she thought the author had done that. . . . Her reply was 'Because . . . at the end they were kind . . . and at the beginning they weren't.' . . . What Ann had was – quite simply – a picture of a book and a ball and her understanding of the story we had shared. The book did not declare the link between theme and illustration, and she had not seen the story before . . . But Ann knew at once that the illustration was a metaphorical representation of reconciliation, or friendship, or what she thought of as 'kindness'.

The Tunnel is full of complexity. For example, the wolf who appears to be taking the form of a tree in the middle of the story is an exact quotation of Crane's wolf in the print of Little Red Riding Hood above the girl's bed. She, too, is dressed in a red cape which echoes the apparel of Little Red Riding Hood. Randomness is evident in the threatening, slightly surreal images that crop up in that terrifying forest. Browne tells us in *The Prose And The Passion* that he often lets his imagination wander in such spreads, little of which is consciously determined. There are fragmented moments in *The Tunnel*, like the little girl's body running with great speed, and plenty of strangeness – the boy's disappearance into the tunnel, the girl's quest through strange and frightening landscapes, the boy turned to stone . . . And at the end, the little girl seems almost to wink at her readers playfully, asking them to conspire with her in appreciating the new-found closeness with her brother.

The Tunnel, it could be argued, like so many picture books produced for young children, is a perfect post-modernist text and one of many in which the readership is entirely at home. Perhaps there is a lesson here for those who subscribe to simple, hierarchical models of literacy development; to those who underestimate the capabilities of young children when engaged on 'work' they find intellectually stimulating, such as interpreting picture books. Then there are those who are more interested in whether children can jump through hoops of correctness in dull exercises from an early age, rather than grapple with young readers on fascinating questions about what the world is like, who they will become when they grow up, why human beings sometimes behave so badly, how this planet is going to survive and what is going to happen at the end of the story. Just watch children confidently absorbed in picture books, laughing with delight, sharing an observation with a friend, turning the page with suspense and wonder and think again.

‘ Children . . . will tolerate ambiguities, peculiarities, and things illogical; will take them into their unconscious and deal with them as best they can. . . . The artist has to be a little bit bewildering and a little bit wild and

44

a little bit disorderly. . . . Artists run into difficulty because they're dealing with our most upright, uptight business, which is the industry called childhood.
'

Maurice Sendak[38]

ACKNOWLEDGEMENT

I should like to thank the Headteacher of St Lukes, Primary School, Cambridge for allowing me to work with the children mentioned in the text. I should like them to know how much they taught me in the few hours we shared picture books together. I have not used the children's real names for the purposes of anonymity.

I am also grateful to Tom Hunter for talking to me about his drawings and letting me use them.

REFERENCES

1 Charlotte Otten, 'An Interview with Maurice Sendak', *Signal 68*, 1992, p. 116.

2 Sheila Egoff, *Thursday's Child.* Chicago, 1981, p. 248.

3 Margaret Meek, 'Novels: Selection', *Signal 1*, 1983.

4 Maurice Sendak, *Caldecott & Co: Notes on Books and Pictures.* London: Viking/Penguin, 1989.

5 Morag Styles and Mary Jane Drummond. *The Politics Of Reading.* Cambridge: Homerton College and University of Cambridge, Institute of Education, 1994; Liz Waterland, *Read With Me.* Stroud: Thimble Press, 1989.

6 David Lewis, 'Looking for Julius: two children and a picture book' in Keith Kimberley *et al.* (eds) *New Readings.* London: A & C Black, 1992, p. 62.

7 Margaret Meek, *How Texts Teach What Readers Learn.* Stroud: Thimble Press, 1988; Judith Graham, *Pictures On The Page.* Sheffield: Nate, 1990; Victor Watson, 'Multilayered Texts, Multilayered Readers' in Morag Styles and Mary Jane Drummond, *The Politics Of Reading*, eds. Cambridge, 1994.

8 Meek 1988, ibid.

9 Hunt, *An Introduction to Children's Literature.* Oxford: University Press. 1994, p. 157.

10 Anthony Browne, *Zoo.* London; Julia MacRae, 1992.

11 Meek, 1988, op. cit.

12 Jan Pienkowski, *Haunted House.* London: Heinemann, 1979.

13 Jon Scieszka and Steve Johnson, *The Frog Prince Continued.* London: Viking, 1991.

14 Peter Hunt, 1994, op. cit. p. 166.

15 David Lewis, in Henrietta Dombey, (ed.) *Literacy for the Twenty-First Century,* Brighton: University of Brighton Press, 1992, p. 81–4.

16 Geoff Moss, 'Metafiction, Illustration, and the Poetics of Children's Literature' in Peter Hunt (ed.) *Literature For Children: Contemporary Criticism.* London: Routledge, 1992, p. 45.

17 Lewis, op. cit., p. 57.

18 Lewis, op. cit.

19 Moss, op. cit., p. 59.

20 Jon Scieszka and Lane Smith, *The True Story Of The Three Little Pigs.* London: Penguin, 1989; Jon Scieszka and Lane Smith, *The Stinky Cheese Man and other fairly stupid tales.* London; Viking, 1992.

21 Jane Doonan, *Signal 64*, 1991, p. 50.

22 Charlotte Otten 'An Interview with Maurice Sendak', *Signal 68*, 1992, p. 125.

23 Hunt, op. cit; p. 171 talking about David McKee, *I Hate My Teddy Bear.* London: Anderson 1982.

24 Anthony Browne, 'Making Picture Books' in Morag Styles, *et al, The Prose And The Passion.* London: Cassell, 1994, pp. 180–5.

25 Moss, op. cit., p. 62.

26 Browne, 1994 op. cit., p. 195.

27 Lewis, op. cit., p. 60.

28 Moss, op. cit., p. 55.

29 Lucy, aged six, is one of Lynda Teichler's pupils at East Tilbury Infants School, Essex. I am grateful to her for permission to quote transcript material. Lynda Teichler was on the Advanced Diploma in Language and Literature at Homerton College, Cambridge.

30 Browne, op. cit., p. 178.

31 Maurice Sendak, *We Are All In The Dumps With Jack And Guy.* New York: Harper Collins, 1993.

32 Jane Doonan, 'Into the Dangerous World' in *Signal 75*, 1994, p. 161.

33 Lucy Pyatt, in an unpublished dissertation for the Education Tripos at Homerton College, 1995.

34 Anthony Browne, *Bear Goes to Town.* London: Hamish Hamilton, 1982.

35 Pyatt, op. cit.

36 Anthony Browne, *The Tunnel*. London: Julia MacRae, 1989.

37 Watson, op. cit.

38 Sendak, 1989 op. cit.

3

Tricks and treats; picture books and forms of comedy

Barbara Jordan

Barbara Jordan considers in some detail how humour works in picture books. Using examples from several of Anthony Browne's outstanding texts and two of Scieszka and Smith's contemporary picture book classics, she demonstrates the complexity of ideas which can be conveyed in graphic form and understood by young readers. Like Morag Styles, in the previous chapter, Barbara Jordan argues that powerful stories involving strong emotions can be handled through pictorial text, because they are also given comic treatment. She goes on to discuss how attuned children are to visual humour: tricks, jokes, visual puns, irony, parody are all taken in their stride and delighted in, partly because of the 'treats' offered by the authors and partly because of their seductive invitations to young readers. Implicit in such texts is a recognition of the subtlety, skill and subversiveness of their intended audience.

Much has been written about picture books over the last fifteen years, including a great deal about how picture books can be used in the process of teaching young learners to read. There are other publications, however, which celebrate the achievements of picture book authors and illustrators in producing beautiful books which are humorous, thought-provoking and sensitive to the interests of children. Picture books are associated with pleasure. They provide a rich experience. They are pleasant to handle, colourful, unpredictable and generally exciting to read. The quality of the books has been rising as parents, teachers, publishers and children come to expect more and more from the book creators. Picture book making is a creative art. There is a constant search for new forms of expression and challenges for the reader. Book makers themselves are continually experimenting, even with the physical form of the book, within the picture book genre. The boundaries of literature, story-telling and humour within books for children are being gently but steadily pushed outwards. These are books which withstand many re-readings and satisfy the need for an engaging story. At their best, picture books bring together meaningful illustration, subtle language, humour and an intellectual challenge for the reader.

To the child, some of the meanings encoded in the picture book text may only be accessible with maturity, but many are available to the youngest of children more readily than to the adult, who may pass too quickly over the fine detail of the illustration. Children become highly sophisticated readers of the graphic form from an early age. They rely upon visual images for most of their understanding. Exposure to the images of television advertising and to print in the environment teaches children that images need decoding and they apply the same process to illustrations in books. In some respects the picture book offers the reader a reflection of contemporary literacy, in that techniques such as freeze-frame, flash-back and close-up, which are the conventions of modern media, are used in the books. These devices are often found, for example, in the work of Shirley Hughes. There are long shots, wide angles, split screens and sometimes the use of a comic-strip format or a backcloth.

Shirley Hughes[1] has commented that:

‹ We are living in an age of visual revolution, one that has been hotted up to lightning speed and is getting quicker all the time. And it is the children who are the sophisticates – and not just in playing video games. Babes whose ages can be measured in months are understanding the image on a page and expecting it to have a relationship to the one on the next! By two they're well into recognising drawing styles. They like this book – they don't like that one! And they want detail. They certainly don't want a lot of primary colours and blank space. ›

Picture books develop children's thinking. They deal with important human issues. Their themes include those areas of life which concern adults as well as children: jealousy, anger, fear, friendship, family relationships and death. Because these aspects of life are complex, the situations in which they are presented are open to interpretation and therefore invite discussion. In this way the books encourage the exploration of moral issues, and help readers to understand differing points of view and come to terms with strong emotions. Children also learn about the aesthetic properties of language from the books. The language has been crafted in highly deliberate ways and stands in a particular relationship to the illustrations. It is language for a specific purpose with a fitness of purpose. It is often spare, leaving the rest of the story to be communicated visually.

Visual art communicates in a great variety of ways. Every mark whether bold, tentative, thick or thin, is telling. The choice of colour and tone creates an emotional mood. The understanding of meaning is not dependent upon there being an actual likeness but is embedded, as children quickly come to know, in the picture's context, its composition and the connotations of the symbols being used. A picture may extend the meaning of the words, but it may also contradict the feeling that is implied, counterpoint the text, complement the words or create an alternative meaning. The illustration may exaggerate irony, express an abstract idea or an emotion or, most importantly, it may be the means of presenting jokes. Humour, which for very young children is heavily dependent upon the visual image, is one of the most widely loved and demanded features of all children's books.

The importance of humour

Visual humour is a characteristic of the work of Anthony Browne. Children learn to look for his visual jokes, for puns, for unusual twists to the text and for metaphors in both written and pictorial form. They know that the pictures will bridge the gaps which the written narrative is unable to fill. Anthony Browne says that he receives more letters from children about *Willy the Wimp*[2] and *Willy the Champ*[3] than about any of his other books or characters. That Willy should have a huge appeal to children is not surprising, but the nature of that appeal, and the ability to draw such a wide response, is of interest and may be related to the humour expressed.

Willy is a likeable character with a gentle and kind nature who is full of self-doubt. In the early illustrations it is obvious that Willy is physically small and underdeveloped. It is tempting to speculate that to a child he represents the aspect of childhood that is experienced through having to grow up in an adult-sized world. Willy is a metaphor for children's own lives. They may be aligning themselves with the hapless Willy who is pushed around by others in a way that children understand because they too are 'pushed around' by the instructions of parents, older siblings, teachers and other adults in authority.

An important attribute of the Willy stories is that they leave the reader with a strong sense of satisfaction. In the end Willy the underdog wins the day. Willy, who obviously represents all that is good and honourable, triumphs over the local bullies through his own efforts and determination. In a simplistic sense it is a story of good over evil, moral values being reasserted, and order being restored to a potentially chaotic situation. It is acceptable and not whimsical only because it is done with exaggerated somewhat 'tongue in cheek' humour.

The satisfactions and delights offered by picture books could be described as 'treats'. According to Wayne Booth [4], characters in fiction allow readers to try on alternative values 'for size' including the trying on of other ways of feeling and behaving. The phrase coined by Booth for this role-play is 'honourable upward hypocrisy'. He suggests that with some ideas and some kinds of characterisation children's first encounters will be in texts rather than in life, as they take on the roles that authors offer them. The treat that is embodied here is in Anthony Browne's ability to allow Willy to become friends with his reader in order that they can share judgements of value. In this situation the reading is, from the child's point of view, rather like a good conversation in which someone else's opinions can be accepted or rejected.

It is important to remember, however, that Willy is not a child. The characters are gorillas, not people and the story is a fantasy, albeit a funny one. The gorillas exhibit the attributes, emotions and behaviour of human beings. It seems we are alert to others of our own kind, that is, creatures who seem to resemble us because they walk upright or can manipulate tools as, for example, monkeys and squirrels can. There is a great fascination in seeing ourselves in fur. In *Willy the Wimp* and *Willy the Champ* there is a rich parade, a pageant, of sporting types and characters from films.

What is particularly engaging about the story is Willy's transformation. One form is enacted on the page, courtesy of Charles Atlas (a joke strictly for a limited audience but not lost on children). Willy sweats and suffers his way through a series of exercises – jogging, boxing, aerobics and weight-training and a specially designed diet until he is physically transformed and can walk down the street with a new self-confidence. The transformation from wimp to hero is irresistible. He becomes Millie's hero. Most importantly for the children, through the final double spread in which he walks into a lamp post and apologises to it, they know it is a trick, an illusion, and that Willy remains essentially the same.

In *Willy the Champ* he tricks Buster Nose, and wins the day. The two elements, transformation and trickery, link Willy into an earlier tradition of humour. The structure behind the story of Willy carries connotations of folk humour in which slapstick is frequently the medium, and parody, particularly of those with wealth or power, is the subject matter. In this tradition the established order is temporarily turned on its head and 'Willy' is king for a day. The parody is usually enacted in costume depicting animals and human characters of symbolic importance. That Willy becomes the Champ is due to his presence of mind and agility, but having 'accidentally' given Buster the equivalent of a knock out punch, Willy says,

> ' 'Oh, I'm sorry,' said Willy, 'are you alright?'
> Buster went home to his mum.[5]   '

Nothing is as it seems at first sight. Buster Nose, who looks so vicious, turns out to be a softy and the unprepossessing but quick-thinking Willy easily tricks him. Of the genesis of *Willy the Wimp* Anthony Browne[6] says:

> ' *Willy the Wimp* was very quick, very light and very easy. The idea for this one came from one or two sources really. It was, to a certain extent, my own childhood. I was a small boy and my father was a big man – he was very physical, he was a professional boxer for part of his life, he was a soldier, he played rugby. He was also gentle and he painted and wrote poems for my brother and me. He encouraged my brother and me to be physical too. So we lifted weights and played rugby and boxed and so on and I always wanted to impress him so I was very influenced by the

Charles Atlas adverts. I also remember hearing Geoffrey Morehouse talking about a trip he made across the Sahara Desert. He wrote a book about it. He very nearly died, he ran out of food and water miles from anywhere and he really thought he was going to die. In the interview he was asked if this had changed him in any way and he said it had. Now when he walks through a crowded street and somebody bumps into him he doesn't say sorry – which is what Willy does. **〉**

Willy the Wimp and *Willy the Champ* are about violence and threatening behaviour being handled in a comic and exaggerated way. As such the stories are likely to have impressed themselves upon many children, for in writing about children's own oral stories Carol Fox[7] found that:

〈 On the whole it is true to say that the stories which most impressed themselves on the children's narrations are the powerful stories, the stories which deal with major fears and strong emotions, however humorously or exotically they are told . . . Violence is a strong theme for all the children, so are birth and death, eating, fights, threatening adults (particularly witches and mothers) and animals or monsters . . . On the whole the children do not tell pretty or dull or sanitized stories but deal in metaphorical form with major fears, such as abondonment, punishment, pain and death, the anger of parents, the jealousy of siblings, loneliness and helplessness. However, the stories are by no means woeful in tone. Often these themes are given comic or exaggerated treatment, and endings tend to be happy. **〉**

It seems that Browne, too, has created stories which deal in strong emotions, contain violence and threatening behaviour, and which present the main character as occasionally helpless and lonely. A significant point made by Carol Fox which is borne out by the success of these books is the importance of tone as an element of appeal to children. The comic and exaggerated treatment works well. Both stories are full of humour, sometimes that generated by an 'innocent' on the loose as in *Willy the Champ* where Willy's triumph includes an element of trickery and luck, and at other times the gentle irony of large gorillas doing aerobics, or the smug posing of the gigantic body builders.

The humour is located in the illustrations, not in the text. Children are naturally highly observant and do not miss the humorous details that

Anthony Browne has embedded in the pictures. It is the humour, operating at a range of levels that also attracts a response from children. They understand visual humour more easily than any other and the book is rich in examples.

The illustrations have unique stylistic characteristics. The figures tend to be drawn in a formal way (compare Shirely Hughes, whose figures appear more flexible and convey a sense of movement on the page). The overall effect is of rigidity and set-piece compositions. Browne indicates movement by extending the colour beyond the outline. In the main, the use of strongly defined, hard-edged, static figures against simple, uncluttered but textured backgrounds serves to concentrate the reader's attention upon the figures. Unusually for Anthony Browne, facial expressions are crucial to reading the ironic meanings and enjoying the humour; Willy's embarrassment at the aerobics class, for instance, or his pride in becoming a hero. There is also an element of caricature running throughout the illustrations which is enhanced through the use of juxtaposition, notably the contrast in size between Willy and the other characters. Anthony Browne's visual humour ranges from the subtlety of a blushing gorilla to the sheer ridiculousness of large gorillas in leotards and legwarmers and the slapstick of Willy walking into a lamp post. Costumes play an important part in making the characters in these books memorable. Willy's trademark is his fairisle sweater. Buster Nose, in contrast, is menacing in his motorcycle leathers and studs, although his sinister appearance is totally undermined by the neat device of a 'smiley' badge on his cap!

The reader is invited to smile ruefully with the skinny, undersized Willy in his desire to be strong. Willy is imbued with an almost Chaplinesque quality in his detachment, his innocence and great desire to please. It is a quality particularly noticeable in *Willy the Champ*, when Willy decides to try cycling and is found lining up with fast, competitive and aggressive racing cyclists who disappear in a blur of colour leaving the ingenuous Willy to pedal sedately on his old-fashioned bike complete with basket on the front. Willy's innocence is repeatedly contrasted with the knowingness of the urban gorillas, the confidence of the body-builders, the 'hunks' at the swimming pool, and his isolation is highlighted by his relationship to these other groups with their well-defined identities. What is transmitted through these images and often depicted through the use of space on the page, is a strong sense of alienation. Willy has individuality but Willy is almost always on his own.

The use of trickery

All kinds of trickery are perpetrated upon the reader by Jon Scieszka and Lane Smith. They assault the reader's senses with colour, striking images and jokes. Within their stories they lay false trails, generate subversive texts and pictures which do not conform to conventional formats and expectations. The stories are also rich in examples of irony, both through words and illustrations.

The True Story of the Three Little Pigs[8] excels as an example of parody, both of the original story and the detective story genre. It is enormously witty and sophisticated. The use of a conversational style of writing gives an impression of familiarity while at the same time being a most challenging kind of text to deal with. The style is akin to oral storytelling, with all the distractions, but in print! It is wholly in keeping with the re-telling of folktales which were originally part of the oral tradition. Folk tales are among the most subversive of texts. They are often concerned with the struggle of the 'underdog' against the force of the establishment; law and order are not always respected, the main protagonists are sometimes tricksters and the rich may have their wealth stolen or be killed. Folk tales can be exciting to read because they contain danger, wrongdoing, surprising and often unpleasant events. In addition, they are complex and unrealistic stories – or so it may seem. But as a metaphor for the adult world, where hostile giants and perilous castles do exist, the folk tales are very realistic. The qualities a character needs to succeed in these stories are those of the trickster – boldness, wit, persistence plus a generous amount of good luck.

The illustrations in Scieszka's and Smith's books echo the tradition of the folk tale in the sense that they are not romantic, sentimental or vague. They have impact. They are sumptuously rich in colour and texture. The books, *The Stinky Cheese Man*[9] and *The True Story of the Three Little Pigs* are about how stories are told and are brilliantly elaborated by Lane

55

Smith's pictures. Both books are packed with exemplars of different visual, textual and graphic techniques. The variety of illustrations, texts and forms of writing gives both books pace. Wit is 'writ large' sometimes literally, throughout the books, as when the reader is at last being presented with 'the real story', and this is emphasised in large capital letters as proof of its authenticity. The pictures present 'larger than life' images. They demand attention. They appear to fill the page with an explosion of paint, collage or ink. *The True Story of the Three Little Pigs*[10] is rich in atmosphere. A period feeling is created through the extensive use of sepia and other brown tones, so that old-fashioned values are linked by association with the wolf. Examples of understatement and wordplay abound, nothing is quite what it seems, especially the wolf, whose true nature and cunning have been cleverly crafted into the language of the story. He is the archetypal trickster with a rational excuse for his behaviour:

> So I went next door to ask if I could borrow a cup of sugar. Now the guy next door was a pig. And he wasn't too bright either,
> he had built his whole house out of straw. Can
> you believe it? I mean, who in his right mind would build a house of straw? So of course the minute I knocked on the door, it fell right in. I didn't want to just walk into someone else's house. So I called,
> "Little pig, little pig, are you in?"
> No answer.
> I was just about to go home without the cup of sugar for my dear old granny's birthday cake.
> That's when my nose started to itch.
> I felt a sneeze coming on.
> Well I huffed.
> And I snuffed.
> And I sneezed a great sneeze.
> And you know what? That whole darn straw house fell down. And right in the middle of the pile of straw was the first little pig – dead as a doornail. He had been home the whole time.[10]

This playful, parodic version of the traditional story expresses an alternative view of the world which appeals to children's imagination and rebelliousness. A subversive text, it successfully fits new meanings into old words in an old story. As new meanings are fitted into the existing form of the folk tale so the boundaries of the form itself develop and change. The

stories in *The Stinky Cheese Man and other fairly stupid tales*[11] are re-
located in the modern world and reflect the culture of advertising, use
modern American idioms and slick narrative style. The book is a
wonderful example of how the traditional fairy story and folk tale can be
subverted. On every level it is anarchic. Most literary and bibliographic
conventions are flouted. The narratives of the original stories –
'Cinderella', 'Little Red Riding Hood', 'The Princess and the Pea' – are
parodied and become 'Cinderumpelstiltskin', 'Little Red Running Shorts',
'The Princess and the Bowling Ball'.

In addition to the subversion of meaning from the original story, this new
version of the story is interactive. The reader is not so much drawn as
propelled into the stories, through a number of devices. One such is the
use of a blank page because one story is cut short when the characters
refuse to cooperate with the narrator who has just pre-empted their story.
The narrator is a protagonist. He addresses the reader directly, he butts in
frequently, and in various dialogues is in fact personified as a little man in
a pointed hat. The narrator has a function, firstly to tell what happened or
what a particular scene was like. This narrator, however, knows more than
the characters know and his function is to manage the successful telling of
stories while gaining the reader's participation through responding to the
story.

In contrast to some of the originals, all these stories are playful and
unpredictable. The humour, in keeping with the folk tale tradition, is
often brusque and shocking but the reader is invited to take it all as a
huge joke. The signals are very clear that this is a world in which anything
goes. The changed story titles, the illustrations which are caricatured,
somewhat surreal, full of exaggeration, significant details and visual puns,
are all indications that the established order does not apply. To emphasise
that in the world of *The Stinky Cheese Man* things may not be what they
seem, many book conventions are turned on their heads. The dedication
page is printed upside down, the print size and style of font varies from
story to story and sometimes within the same story and a page is left blank
(compare *Tristram Shandy* in which Laurence Stern invites the reader to
write on the empty page.[12]) There is cross-referencing and quotation
between stories in both the text and illustrations, for example, the giant,
who appears in 'Jack's Bean Problem' also appears outside the window in

the Cinderumpelstiltskin illustration. In the final picture the giant reappears and it is inferred that he has eaten Little Red Hen, who has been portrayed as an irate, demanding, irascible tyrant throughout the book. There are feathers floating on the page, two hen's legs appear to be sticking out of the giant's mouth, the hen's tell-tale blue bonnet is to be seen, but no sign of the hen. The construction of the book allows characters to weave in and out of the stories – Little Red Hen, in particular, is very pushy in trying to get her story told and appears at various points in the narrative. The giant, too, appears several times and we are requested not to wake him at the end. The 'hair' from 'The Tortoise and the Hair' story is literally drawn over the page and into the next story and becomes entwined into the first word.

Just as complexity of meaning is found in the relationship and interplay between the text and illustrations, so the same combination makes possible many varieties of humour. In this case a clever and sophisticated parody has been produced. But what do children understand of it? How many children may, when encountering this form of text, recognise that reference is being made to other literature, but only that? To return to Wayne Booth[13] for a moment – if parody is the form of 'honourable upward hypocrisy' that children meet, what are the implications for the young reader? In the case of folk tales the stories are already removed from their original contexts and in parody they are two steps removed. Are there any dangers in meeting the parody before reading the original story, given that parody is utterly dependent for its effect on the reader's knowledge of other texts?

The work of Propp[14] on genres indicates that some forms of story such as folk and fairy tales can be reduced to a set of basic structural units. The actions (functions) of the characters in the stories remain constant and can be grouped together and categorised into elements such as 'departure'. When Propp analysed the functions in one hundred Russian fairy stories he found that the actions in all the tales could be accounted for in thirty-one elements. The fundamental structural base for these stories is shared around the world; it is basic but strong enough to survive many forms of adaptation, including parody.

Carol Fox believes that in listening to their favourite stories children hear metaphors for their own concerns, their own emotions and their own lives. The children in her study often make use of traditional stories, particularly fairy tales, to disguise and make manageable the major concerns in their stories. The children use versions of the fairy tale form more than any other. Their own stories incorporate, in verbal form, many of the devices being used by Scieszka and Smith in written form. The children's narratives contain jokes, they parody and make fun of various characters. Noises, whistles, funny voices and songs are often incorporated into the telling. Exaggeration is a recurring feature of the storying and their story worlds are 'inhabited by invented characters and animals including lions, bears, rabbits, monkeys, witches, giants, robbers, policemen, heartless mothers and small children.'[15] From the fairy-tale tradition the children borrow the use of magic and coincidence. Violence is frequently included and the children use the technique of building up fear and suspense. Extreme forms of punishment are also a feature of the narrative.

The permanent tradition of folk humour has always included pageants, processions, parodies and humorous satirical plays. Traditionally it contains a strong element of play and the characters involved celebrate temporary liberation from the prevailing truth with sensuousness. It offers an opportunity for subverting established social order and as parody for subverting officially sanctioned meanings.

The last word goes to Jack as he tries to get his story told in 'Jack's Bean Problem.'[16]

‘ "Forget that hen.
Now it's time for the best story in the whole book – my story.
Because Once Upon a Time I traded our last cow for three magic beans
and . . . hey, Giant. What are you doing down here? You're wrecking my
whole story."
'I DON'T LIKE THAT STORY" said the Giant. "YOU ALWAYS TRICK
ME."
"That's the best part," said Jack.
"FEE FI FUM FORY I HAVE MADE MY OWN STORY."
"Great rhyme, Giant. And I'm sure your story is just as good. But there's
no room for it. So why don't you climb back up the beanstalk. I'll be up in
a few minutes to steal your gold and your singing harp."

"I'LL GRIND YOUR BONES TO MAKE MY BREAD."
"I knew you'd understand. And there's another little thing that's been bugging me. Could you please stop talking in uppercase letters? It really messes up the page."
"I WILL READ MY STORY NOW," said the Giant. And he did.   ,

REFERENCES

1 Shirley Hughes. *Times Educational Supplement*, 27 May, 1994.

2 Anthony Browne, *Willy the Wimp*. London: Little Mammoth, 1984.

3 Anthony Browne, *Willy the Champ*. London: Little Mammoth, 1985.

4 Wayne Booth, discussed in Morag Styles, Eve Bearne and Victor Watson, *After Alice: Exploring Children's Literature*. London: Cassell, 1992, p. 148.

5 Anthony Browne, op. cit.

6 Anthony Browne, 'Making Picture Books', in Morag Styles, Eve Bearne and Victor Watson, *The Prose and the Passion: Children and their Reading*. London: Cassell, 1994, pp. 191–2.

7 Carol Fox, *At the Very Edge of the Forest: The Influence of Literature on the Storytelling of Children*. London: Cassell, 1993, pp. 21–2.

8 Jon Scieszka and Lane Smith, *The True Story of the Three Little Pigs*. London: Penguin, 1991.

9 John Scieszka and Lane Smith, *The Stinky Cheese Man and other fairly stupid tales*. London: Viking, 1992.

10 Jon Scieszka and Lane Smith, 1991, op. cit.

11 Jon Scieszka and Lane Smith, 1992, op. cit.

12 Laurence Sterne, *Tristram Shandy*, first published 1760–7.

13 Wayne Booth, op. cit.

14 Vladimir Propp, *The Morphology of the Folk Tale*. Texas: University of Texas Press, 1928.

15 Carol Fox, op. cit.

16 Jon Scieszka and Lane Smith, 1992, op. cit.

Reading picture books with an artist's eye

Helen Gomez-Reino

....

Helen Gomez-Reino was an Art History student teacher in her final year at Homerton College when she wrote a discerning essay on picture books for the Education Tripos. It was seized upon by the editors of this book for its originality and fine artistic perspective, and it wasn't long before Helen was persuaded to adapt the piece for this publication. Clearly influenced by the work of Jane Doonan, Helen makes original and independent judgements about some of her favourite artists and, in non-technical language, draws the reader into a greater understanding of how pictorial texts can literally be read 'with an artist's eye'. Like Helen Bromley, in Chapter 7, this writer believes that children, as well as adults, can appreciate and draw on artistic knowledge and art history in responding to picture books. Helen, and others like her, are pushing back the frontiers of what teachers can expect of children in classrooms where care, attention and time are devoted to artistic as well as literary conventions, and where there is a recognition that the reading of picture books, like other modes of reading, is capable of being extended and developed.

An artist's approach to picture books offers a professional and distinctive perspective. The artist has an understanding of technicalities, such as the nature of the media used, the nature of the line, and how the shapes or colours are organised. Artists also bring to their work a knowledge of art history. Maurice Sendak[1] once described the execution of an artistic idea 'You get the idea . . . and then you construct a form, words, pictures, the shape of the book, the binding, the cover. Everything.' Sendak's strong belief in the unity of the artist's thought is illuminating: we too should look at a picture book as a whole entity shaped by words and aesthetic elements. Or, as Jane Doonan suggests[2]

'Pictures are made of simple basic ingredients: arrangements of interwoven lines and shapes and colours which the artist sets down in a particular medium and, at the same time, organises.'

Picture books can convey strong ideas, explore difficult feelings, offer ambiguous meanings and raise uncomfortable issues in many different ways. If we are to understand such complexity, we must approach a picture book with a readiness to appreciate the unity of all its features. For example, in *Jyoti's Journey* by Helen Ganly[3], a young Indian girl comes to England to join her father who has found a job in a town. The written story is quite direct and concise in that it tells the events that are involved in everyday living in India, leaving her home country and arriving in another one where everything is new and grey. The point to make here is the importance of the visual representation: Ganly uses collage in a way which adds impact and depth to the meaning.

After many hours they arrived at the airport. They had to wait for a very long time before they were allowed to join father. They were tired.

Figure 6 From *Jyoti's Journey* by Helen Ganley, published by André Deutsch

Her depiction of India emphasises the richness of the shapes and colours which surround Jyoti, who radiates happiness and seems to belong to a wide polychromatic whole. Using collage serves the purpose well, as the little girl is like a single piece of the rich puzzle in a country such as India. Once that piece is placed in a completely different context (or against a grey, uniform, monotonous background) the conflict begins. It shows the isolation of a small figure against a new and forced context. The visual shock of such a change of scene is cleverly achieved through the use of collage. The choice of colours, warm or cold, and the patterns and shapes, are related to the feelings aroused by this dramatic disturbance.

Reading pictures can be as easy or difficult as reading printed text. Illustrations within a picture book can vary as much as styles of writing. Take *Piggybook* by Anthony Browne.[4] Browne shapes the written text with description as well as dialogue. He makes use of short, concise sentences, mirroring the style of his illustrations which have sharp and defined contour lines. The changing events described in *Piggybook* occur against the shifting imagery of metamorphosis. The language used is as direct and explicit as the images portrayed. The protagonists in the story are illustrated in realistic detail which brings the content closer to the reader's every-day life and experiences. The artistic techniques employed by Browne have specific objectives. For example, the colour and line in the scenes where the mother is shown doing all the house-work convey a feeling of isolation, dullness and, perhaps, alienation. The colour is grey. The faceless mother is portrayed as a victim. To achieve this purpose Browne presents her smaller in scale than her pig-like husband. This is clearly the case in the illustration where half the father's face appears in contrast to the four representations of the mother depicted in miserable drudgery (see figure 7).

Sharp, carefully defined lines shape the hideous figures of the father and the two sons, as they metamorphosise into pigs in opposition to the considerably more blurred and soft images through which the mother appears.

Another author whose works include semi-fantastic and semi-real overlaps is Sendak. In *Where the Wild Things Are*[5], the transition between the real world (Max's bedroom) and his own imaginary world (the place where

63

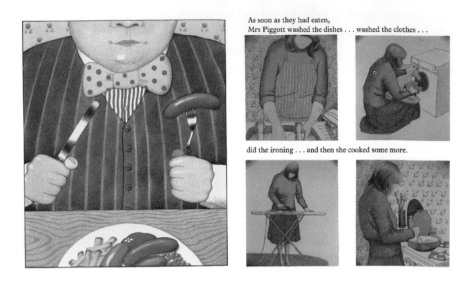

Figure 7 **From *Piggybook* by Anthony Browne, published by Julia MacRae Books**

the wild things are) is gradually introduced with long narrative sentences and the growing format of the illustrations. This is another example of a story involving an initial everyday scene, a naughty boy making mischief, which becomes the starting point to a fantastic voyage. These happenings acquire a type of timeless quality with the dark use of the line (cross-hatching and hatching) which has the quality of a print. The colours seem to become brighter with the reduction of the line when Max sets off on his wild dream. The grey effect of the initial illustrations is gradually substituted in order to adjust to the more lively and active events going on. The cross-hatching is mainly restricted to Max and the Wild Things in order to shape their bodies whether in motion or not. This dynamic and expressive use of line in Sendak's work is quite different from that of Browne, though both illustrators achieve powerful results.

In some books for young readers illustration is the only 'text'. Take *Anno's Journey* by Mitsumaso Anno.[6] This is a multilayered text where the drawings are executed with great care and delicacy. Firstly, one might notice that the equestrian figure of Anno appears in each of the different scenes, so the book becomes a type of game in which the young reader is challenged to look and find. The viewer might then begin to scrutinise all the detail offered by the various buildings, figures, animals, trees, fields. On a further reading, the richness of expression, gesture and movement might be noticed. For instance, each group of people and buildings tells a different story.

Anno's use of line is his most significant form of expression. The thin ink pen has been employed in ways that remind us of a print by Durer and the onlooker is enchanted by the complementary use of meticulous contour lines and soft colour. Then there is the eclectic nature of the book. Another layer reveals reference to real works of art and the artists who might have influenced Anno while he was composing this book. For example, Anno 'quotes' from paintings by some Realistic artists such as Courbet and Millet, and some Pointillists such as Georges Seurat. On the one hand, the overall effect is not far from being a 'Realistic'

Figure 8 **From *Anno's Journey* by Mitsumaso Anno, published by Fukuinkan Shoten Publishers, Inc., Tokyo**

representation of everyday life in Northern Europe; on the other hand it owes much to the delicate and volatile atmosphere created by artists such as Signac and Seurat.

The intertextuality in *Anno's Journey* is taken further by the introduction of other stories: Pinocchio, Don Quixote, Little Red Riding Hood; children's street games, musical representation (Beethoven's Ninth Sympony), and characters from television such as the Sesame Street puppets. Mitsumasa Anno has included all these disparate elements in a single picture book in a skilful and unifying manner. Although a child is unlikely to know Courbet's *Stone Breakers* or Seurat's *Bathers*, reference to these paintings add to the satisfactions implicitly available in the illustrations. These extra dimensions are available for more sophisticated readers or when less experienced readers revisit favourite picture books. Many commentators have suggested that picture books have been judged too much as works of literature and not nearly enough as works of visual art. As Helen Bromley argues in Chapter 7, children *are* interested in the artistic aspects of intertextuality, such as allusions to or quotations from famous artists.

In *Through The Window* by Charles Keeping[7] a succession of everyday incidents is seen through the window, from a child's point of view. The cover and the title page, as well as the end-papers, introduce us to the world of texture and colour seen through a child's eyes. The effect is quite dramatic. The enclosed frame, within which the diverse scenes are presented, is introduced on the front cover. The netted curtains which appear throughout the story, frame not only the child's head, but his enquiring thoughts and feelings when viewing people and animals as they pass by.

The presence of Jacob, the central character, can be perceived in all the pictures, even those in which his head does not appear. That is, the curtains become a personification of Jacob. The dripping ink, the irregular strokes, and the various patches of colour, give us an extraordinary insight into a small person's view of reality. By depicting this evolution of events in such an original way, Keeping reinforces the idea that a child's experience is quite different from that of an adult by the simple device of leaving the child on his own in his front room interpreting ordinary events. The colouring and style used by Keeping create a mood of loneliness and stillness. On each page the author selects a range of colours with one predominant. For example, the initial scene with the faceless Jacob, is represented in what Whistler might have named a 'Harmony in Yellow/Orange'. Each page is coloured in a similar way, which makes them individual, yet unified. The irregular and determined use of line, as well as the sharp contrast of light and dark, are exploited to achieve great dynamism, whether expressed in open movement or not. Jacob is the witness of a changing and mysterious world, which triggers strong feelings in him. These are clearly conveyed through the dramatic use of inks.

In *Angry Arthur* by Satoshi Kitamura[8], Arthur is not allowed to watch the television. As a result he becomes extremely angry. His disproportionate response is conveyed through his distorted view of the reality around him. That is, the choice of colours, shapes, and most of all, the perspectives gives Arthur's anger an unreal and fantastic dimension. Objects,

Arthur's country and Arthur's town, his street, his house, his garden and his bedroom

Figure 9 **From *Angry Arthur* by Satoshi Kitamura, published by Andersen Press**

buildings, streets and plants appear to echo the effects of his destructive anger. The outburst of energy is reflected through the use of broken, angular lines. The irregularity of the clearly defined shapes contrasts with the watercolour background. The subtle tonal changes in the consistency of the paint make the world around Arthur expand and shrink to nothingness, especially towards the end of the story. To achieve this effect Kitamura does not include conventional frames surrounding each illustration. The various scenes within the book are, therefore, not limited by any enclosing lines which might become an obstacle to the fantastic and extreme story. The effects of Arthur's anger go beyond the white page and perspective emphasises this still further. The reader is led into each scene through different viewpoints which vary in inclination. The presentation of each illustration includes the viewer quite openly and that is how Arthur's world becomes part of the reader's world. This effect can be further explained by the inclusion in most cases of half cut-off figures, objects, buildings and so forth, which seem to seek a place in the reader's own world.

The colouring throughout emphasises the dynamic and destructive power of Arthur's anger. Purples, blues, pinks are made to surround Arthur's world, shaping it as a magic scenery where chaos takes place. Such colours provide a powerful and yet fragile base of semi-transparent tones which confirm this exaggerated view of a child's tantrum. The inconsistency and irregularity in the presentation of each illustration makes Arthur's anger grow in an extreme and unpredictable manner.

The True Story of The Three Little Pigs as told by Jon Scieszka[9] adds much to the conventional presentation of a tale.[9] 'Everybody knows the story of the Three Little Pigs. Or at least they think they do.' The Daily Wolf describes through both written text and images the wolf's version of the well-known story. The yellow tinted pages reinforce the fact that the illustrations of events shape an old story which has been misread and filed away for quite some time.

The newspaper format gives the narration of events a quality of realism which is picked up in some illustrations within the story. The blurred overall impression of each picture is like a 'flash-back'. In order to achieve this quasi-real effect Lane Smith generally avoids the use of well-defined

The rest, as they say, is history.

he news reporters found out about the two pigs I had for dinner. They figured a sick guy going to borrow a cup of sugar didn't sound very exciting. So they jazzed up the story with all of that "Huff and puff and blow your house down." And they made me the Big Bad Wolf.

That's it.
The real story. I was framed.

Figure 10 **From *The True Story of the Three Little Pigs* by Jon Scieszka, published by Penguin**

lines and contours which shape the memory of Alexander T. Wolf when recalling his unfortunate fate. This hazy recollection of events is made more unreal and inconcrete through the choice of subtle colours such as ochres, browns, and deep greens.

Lane Smith becomes experimental in his use of pigment as well as in his selection of the elements included in each illustration. The modernised text seems to be mirrored in the images with the inclusion of cuttings from real photographs, enhancing the overall surreal impression. Each composition is distorted or awkward, depending on the point of view. There are wide images of scenes, as well as 'close-ups' which add dynamism and new life to the retold story. Both written and pictorial texts are innovative and surprising. For instance, some of the figures go beyond the frame, including the picture of the wolf in the front cover. In doing this, the illustrator establishes that the boundaries between what is thought to be real (newspaper article), and what is fantasy (story), can be easily confused and misinterpreted. The humanised image of Alexander

T. Wolf with his spectacles on the front cover suggests an ambiguity between this 'realistic' version of a well-known story and the 'invented' traditional narration.

I have tried to demonstrate that the effects achieved through the particular use of media in some picture books are integrally related to the written text. They complement each other to provide an artistic whole. Collage, inks, water-colours and pencils are used for different purposes in picture books to execute and develop particular ideas, moods and impressions. To assume that the image is a mere representation or visualisation of the written word is to miss the complexity that is to be found in quality picture books. Images can be used in diverse ways as vehicles of communication for intimate and personal messages, and this leads to an exchange which takes place between the adults who create and the children who read, making powerful and meaningful texts. Although children may not be familiar with the 'grammar' of painting, it seems likely that many can approach picture books with an artist's eye. How they develop the artist's eye – or whether they had it from the beginning – is another story.

REFERENCES

1 Maurice Sendak, *Caldecott and Co: Notes on Books and Pictures*. London: Viking Penguin, 1989.

2 Jane Doonan, *Looking at Pictures in Picture Books*. Stroud: Thimble Press, 1992.

3 Helen Ganly, *Jyoti's Journey*. London: André Deutsch, 1986.

4 Anthony Browne, *Piggybook*. London: Julia MacRae, 1986.

5 Maurice Sendak, *Where the Wild Things Are*. London: Bodley Head, 1967.

6 Mitsumaso Anno, *Anno's Journey*. London: Bodley Head, 1978.

7 Charles Keeping, *Through the Window*. Oxford: Oxford University Press, 1970.

8 Satoshi Kitamura, *Angry Arthur*. London: Andersen Press, 1982.

9 Jon Scieszka and Lane Smith, *The True Story of the Three Little Pigs*. London: Penguin, 1989.

5

Getting into the picture

••

Shirley Hughes

**Most of the contributors to this book make homage at some point to
the work of Shirley Hughes. She is quite simply one of the finest children's illustrators and someone who clearly respects her young readership. It is a great treat to get a chance to hear Shirley Hughes' own
voice, as well as to see spreads of some beautiful artwork for
Enchantment in the Garden which had not been published at the
time *Talking Pictures* was being put together. Shirley Hughes shares
some of the secrets of her craft, letting us in on how she manages to
evoke Italian gardens in summer in her West London studio on a
bleak day, or how she consciously works to involve the young reader
in her illustrations. And, like Helen Bromley in a later chapter, she
takes us back to the history of narrative painting. Shirley Hughes has
firm views on the importance of good draughtmanship, and explains
some of the technicalities involved in producing a picture book. Best
of all, she helps the reader to 'get into the picture', using words
instead of brush strokes, on this occasion.**

It is around 9.30 am and I am in my workroom, poised over a double-
page colour illustration for my new book. The light is fine, thank
goodness (I hate having to turn on the lamp as I need natural light to get
the colour values right.) This is the finished stuff, the Real McCoy, the
one which, with the rest of the set, will eventually travel to Hong Kong or
Vicenza or some such place to be printed, bound and made into a sixty-
four-page picture book. Irrevocable commitment. Mistakes, if there are
any, irredeemable.

This is not a relaxing thought so I don't dwell on it. At this stage I am not
thinking about the reader either. That was way back when I was plotting
the story, writing and re-writing the text. This one is not an 'Alfie' book,
but a magic story set in Italy in the 1920s – very operatic, with a statue

who comes to life, Renaissance gardens, moonlit balcony scenes and so forth. It draws on sketch books and illustrated diaries which I have made for my own amusement on many trips to Tuscany, Umbria and Rome. These sketchbooks lie open all over the workroom. They help to carry me out of the cool light of West London, back to a spot under a tree on a sunny terrace, a glass of Chianti at hand, attempting to record violet shadows, ochre-washed walls, flower pots overflowing with geraniums, and beyond, hazily seen, the most ravishing of all landscapes.

The keeping of sketchbooks is not only to have a reminder of past journeys and happy tours; they are a life-line for achieving some kind of freedom of technique. Illustrating a book is an exacting business – you are committed to producing not one picture which says everything about a particular moment in time, as a landscape painter does, but a whole series of connected imagined images which relate strongly to one another. As such, they must carry a lot of specific information and descriptive characterisation if they are to hold the narrative. They must involve a reader, especially one who may not yet be able to decipher the text, and invite him or her to turn the page and find out what happens next. But with sketchbooks I feel unfettered by the demands of a text or of attention to careful finish. I can make as many mistakes as I like, scribble over things, experiment with colour, react to the moment, observe people chatting in bars or lounging in parks. It is a kind of on-going limbering up process for when I am back in the workroom, and, even more importantly, an invaluable training for the visual memory.

The illustrations I am working on call for a particularly high degree of freedom in the brushwork. With colour I work tonally – that is, I aim to achieve a three-dimensional quality of depth, to open up the page from foreground to middle distance and beyond so the reader can enter the scene, perhaps even fantasise about what is not in the frame but around the corner. For the finished pictures I use chalks combined with colour washes – gouache, which is similar to water colour but has a bit more body. The washes go on in layers, solidifying towards the foreground. The underlying drawing disappears under these washes but I bring it back again at the final stages with very fine brushes. It is perilously easy to overwork this process along the way – and thus lose the spontaneity. I imagine it's rather like playing jazz; I do often play a tape of virtuoso instrumentalists like Lester Young or Benny Goodman while working – you are endlessly taking risks, exploiting the happy accident. But all the time riding on a carefully controlled technique.

I have always had a strong conviction (at times unfashionably) that in our job good draughtsmanship underpins even the most uninhibited colour technique. Without it everything falls apart and the younger 'reader' cannot follow the story. But photographic realism will not do on its own. We are, amongst other things, trying to entice children (and adults) who are steeped from the cradle in moving photographic imagery, to make their own personal, leisurely exploration of a picture. Even to perceive the difference between a drawing and a photograph. It is no good, either, simply cramming the frame with visual information, all of which is given equal emphasis. A picture book is a drama. We aim to lead the eye to the bit of the stage where the main action is taking place, to highlight a telling gesture, a touching facial expression or an important detail tucked in somewhere which is a vital clue to the plot.

When work is going well and I have got hold of a brush which is just right and the washes are flowing sweetly, daily concerns and family cares go quite out of my mind. Even though I know I haven't a hope of re-creating the vision which is in my head, it's still the nearest thing I know to flying into the sun. The linchpin to everything, of course, is the rough dummy. I hang onto it all the way. I have made it, carefully amended it, talked it over at length with my editor, at least six months or maybe a year before getting into the finished artwork. It is the essence of the book. The pattern of each page is arrived at by arranging blocks of text (hand-written at this stage) and drawing rough sketches around them so they work together as a whole. Each spread has its own requirements, dictated by the structure of the story. I do them on very smooth paper which I can just see through so that I can place one spread over another and compare them. I draw in pencil and go over it with a fine-line felt pen which gives a good clear photocopy. These first drawings, not surprisingly, have a freedom and economy of gesture which is quite hard to reproduce all over again when it comes to the finished colour work. Making these first roughs, drawing very rapidly in a state of high excitement, I am very unselfconscious. Tapping into this freedom and translating it successfully is perhaps one of the great tests of professionalism.

If my story centres on a character like Alfie or, as in a recent book, his little sister Annie Rose, I always find myself concentrating on *their* concentration – that total, all-out single-mindedness with which children of this age address the matter in hand, and the utter consternation which sometimes ensues if things go wrong. With this kind of realistic drama it is important to try to draw with the kind of vitality which convinces your audience that you are drawing from life. This particular family, this home and street, this somewhat chaotic domestic clutter, gives the reader an opportunity to identify strongly with the action. But in fact I make it all up.

There is plenty of real-life data right outside my window in the communal garden square where children come out to play after school (as mine once did). They hop, skip, jump, get up impromptu games and fool around in ways which, in spite of more sophisticated entertainments, still seem to be perennial. But when it comes to creating fictional characters I never use real models. Alfie and co. are not taken from my own children at that age or anyone else's – though inspired by a combination of both.

Very young readers enjoy seeing a world which is highly recognisable. With a series like the 'Alfie' books (though I had no idea when I did the first story that this is what it might become) it is important to build on detail and reassuring familiarity. Yet at the same time I find that with each book I am telling the reader a little more about this imaginary, but to them I hope, very 'real' world. I hold a whole lot of visual data about Alfie and Annie Rose's home, their street, their friends and relations in my head. I will probably use it all, bit by bit. I like the idea of opening out from the minutiae of life – stones, leaves, much loved old toys, mud, conkers – to the wide horizons, the moon, the sea, the clouds. Small children are inevitably home-based, often town-based. Their intense concentration on the detail of things and astonishing visual memory is part of this constricted vision. This can, I sometimes fear, be damaged by having their visual responses hotted up to a lightning pace. One has this passionate desire to slow this down, to get them to look around with eyes wide open. The colours 'out there', even if viewed with a foreground of chimney pots and TV aerials, are still stunningly beautiful.

There is an audience who is beginning to move on from the picture story-book stage, for which 'Dogger' and the 'Alfie' books are designed, and who is ready for something a bit more adventurous in the combination of word and image. Being already highly visually literate, these readers can use this skilled response as a springboard into poetry or more advanced fiction.

The book I am currently working on (*Enchantment in the Garden* to be published by Bodley Head/Random House, in 1996) inhabits the wilder shores of my imagination. The design of the page is crucial to the telling of the story. The needs of the narrative determine how it will look. I have always wanted to tell a romantic story which boys can enjoy as well as girls. The pressure to be gunslingers and avengers at an early age does seem sadly regrettable. With this book I needed the page to open up like a stage set (see figures 11 to 13). The slightly longer text needed to be spaciously accommodated. After experimenting with different formats I found that I could put all the typesetting into tall upright panels and move them about like the screens in a Japanese NO play, signalling shifts in time and perspective, close-up and long shot. Each panel could then have its own separate line drawing dropped in as a further commentary on the cast of characters. Then, to my delight, it was possible to design a book lavishly illustrated in both colour and line, a throw-back to the thrill of those glamorous Rackham and Dulac giftbooks which I pored over as a child.

The borderline, or market, for picture books is now being rapidly expanded up the age range – which is as it should be. Narrative painting goes back a very long way. It flourished at a time when only a small élite of the population could read and all artists were required to use their skills to communicate the stories of the Bible to a largely unlettered audience. Now, in the late-twentieth century, when 'mainstream' art has moved more and more away from narrative towards the conceptual, a large chunk of the population is thus excluded.

Figures 11, 12 and 13 These are roughs of three double-page spreads for *Enchantment in the Garden*. Shirley Hughes explains: 'The tall upright panels are moved about like screens against a backdrop of rioting colour. There are small drop-in drawings printed in line in each panel. See over

Sometimes she and Valerie had tea together and played dance records on the gramophone. In between whiles she lay with her eyes half closed on a sofa in the dim, lofty salon.

Valerie was an only child. She was too serious for her age and had more toys and dresses than she could possibly need. But she had few friends and, of course, she was lonely.

Valerie's father was a rich man. He owned hotels and restaurants all over Italy and was often away from home, looking after his business interests.

Her mother was a beautiful American lady. She breakfasted late, long after Valerie had started her lessons, then drove out to meet her friends for lunch. In the evening she put on an elegant dress, covered in sparkling beads, and went to balls and parties.

Figure 11

No one could decide what was to be done with Cherubino. A search was made for parents or relatives but none could be found. Cherubino had Gained the power of speech when Valerie had brought him to life. But when he tried to explain that he was two and a half thousand years old, and that he had been carved by a Greek sculptor in Southern Italy, dug up in the fifteenth century, purchased by a merchant Prince and put in the Gardens, naturally nobody believed him.

In the end they took him to an orphanage and put him into the care of the nuns in the hope that he would be cured of telling such wicked lies.

A boy in the garden with next to no clothes on! Whatever next?

People came running. They covered Cherubino with scarves and coats and hustled him away, scolding and bombarding him with questions.

Nobody paid the least attention to Valerie as she ran behind, pulling the unwilling Miss McKenzie with her and shouting out:

'But he's Cherubino, I tell you! He's one of the gods of the garden!'

Figure 12

Everyone in the house was asleep when Valerie was woken by tiny pebbles thrown against her shutters. She crept out onto her balcony and saw him standing there in the hot still garden. The moon was making shadows from the leaves; ripple all over him like water.

Figure 13

78

I realise that, largely by accident, I had the ideal upbringing for an illustrator. For a pre-television child the Sunday afternoon outing, if you were lucky, was a trip to an art gallery. In my case it was the Walker in Liverpool or the Port Sunlight collection, both of which were packed with late Victorian narrative paintings such as 'When did you last see your Father?' and S. J. Soloman's 'Samson'. Though illustrators co-exist and are influenced by new visual languages – we all use film syntax and feed off strip cartoon one way or another – the central challenge still is to try to attract someone into a narrative through their pleasure in the imagery. After all, what could be more interactive than a picture book?

Imaginationing *Granpa* – journeying into reading with John Burningham

Victor Watson

Victor Watson's patience and skill with small children is rewarded in this insightful chapter where he documents two little girls reading John Burningham's *Granpa*. His own reading of this outstanding text is sensitive, original and, at times, poetic and, like Morag Styles, he is interested in it as a post-modernist text. The transcripts of his conversations with the children and his attempts to understand their thinking open a window for us on *how* young readers interpret ideas and themes in picture books. Instead of discounting what seems like light-hearted giggling, Victor Watson is alert to why the girls might be behaving in an apparently frivolous way about a serious text. In a brilliant ending, he suggests that the girls were echoing the language and attitudes of the little girl in *Granpa*, (who was about their age), which gives some indication of the authenticity of Burningham's portrayal of childhood.

On my regular visits to a local Infants' School, I took with me a large box of picture books and allowed readers to choose whatever interested them. John Burningham's *Granpa*[1] was not a regular favourite like *Peace at Last*[2], or *Rosie's Walk*[3], or *Up and Up*[4], but it was sometimes chosen, though rarely for a second time. *Granpa* provides none of the supports that new readers seize upon – repetitions and refrains, pantomimic action, jokes and surprises, or phonic word-patterning – and it goes further even than Burningham's other picture books in what David Lewis has called its 'close contact with the unfinished and incomplete nature of contemporary life.'[5] Adult readers have seen in *Granpa* the supreme example of a post-modernist picture book, and I had already found that it evoked in young readers an unusually complex and attentive response. This chapter is an attempt to analyse one example of that

80

complexity, when Ann and Sadie, who usually read separately with me came together one afternoon and happened to choose *Granpa*. They were six years old. (See also Chapters **8** and **11**.)

I might as well confess at once that I found that the misunderstandings and discontinuities within the text seemed in a rather eerie way to extend beyond it. For example, Sadie, looking at the seaside picture, kept saying 'Look, pigs! Pigs! Pigs!' When I spoke sharply to her, poor Sadie expressed a strong sense of injustice, for she had been saying *pegs* – and yet it was hardly surprising that I had made the mistake, as shortly before that Ann had been making pig-snorting noises! 'That was not a nice noise to make,' I might have said – and 'That was not a nice thing to say to Sadie,' she might have retorted. Of course, we did not say those things; such close parallelism between texts and life rarely occurs. But there did seem to be *some* kind of parallelism at work – and it is that phenomenon that I wish to explore.

Granpa is like reading our own experience; it involves making coherence out of existential scraps. The book is about a culture and how a child learns its practices; it *enacts* the mystifications of learning. It is about making meaning, not made meaning. Perhaps it is not surprising that the responses of two six-year-old readers, encountering this book for the first time, should be disorderly, uncertain and exploratory. To put it another way, a post-modernist text seemed to have made Sadie and Ann into post-modernist readers.[6]

Granpa is about an old man's past as well as a little girl's present. She is part of a continuity which reveals itself in fragments and opens out *backwards*, ultimately in the final picture suggesting that the past and the future are capable of some kind of magical, or conceptual, convergence. Granpa is innocent of didactic intentions but he nevertheless passes on to the little girl seminal cultural scraps which become part of her complex and often ambiguous learning. She learns about playing in summer back gardens, about the past, about the strange cultural practices associated with 'a day at the seaside', about sexual embarrassment, and that adults can be hurt. And she learns about love. She presumably makes her own structure of these fragments but, since readers are told nothing of either the process or the product, they must do the work themselves.

81

Ann and Sadie found no difficulty in the first opening: the words teach
the first-time reader that this typeface is for Granpa's words, and the two
figures show through body posture and facial expression their happiness
and mutual welcoming. But when we turn over we find a different kind of
opening, full of puzzling disconnectedness. There are four elements here:
the illustration of the two of them in Granpa's greenhouse, his comment
(which seems to be an answer to an 'absent' question), the girl's
subsequent enquiry about worms in heaven, and the sepia drawing of a
greenhouse-staging with pots, seed-trays, watering-can, and so on. This is
where the hard work begins; readers have to make some sense of how
these elements relate to one another. None of the children I have shared
this book with has found this difficult. All have immediately 'known' that
the sepia drawing represents what Granpa is thinking, or what the little
girl is thinking. One boy said he knew this was so because 'thoughts don't
have colours'.

And how's my little girl?

Figure 14 From *Granpa* by John Burningham, published by Jonathan Cape

Commentators have been inclined to assume that these sepia drawings
always represent Granpa's thoughts. But young readers often read them
differently. In the next opening, the drawing shows three small children
singing beside a man playing an upright piano (figure 15). There are
visual clues – the aspidistra, the man's waistcoat with back buckle – which
suggest a long-ago period, but young readers see no reason why this sketch
should not represent the little girl's imagined picture of Granpa's
childhood. Judith Graham says of this picture book: 'Every illustration is
fed by an earlier or later one'.[7] This is true, and it applies to dialogue as
well, for the children in the illustration are probably the 'Harry, Florence
and I' that Granpa refers to later. But the first-time reader cannot know
that. Meanwhile on the opposite page more cultural learning is going on:
the girl watches Granpa singing and copies his rather stagey operatic
gestures.

But whose is the sepia drawing in the next opening? (See figure 16.) Here
we have Granpa giving his grandchild a sharp lesson in sexual
embarrassment. We do not know precisely what has happened but we can

One man went to mow
Went to mow a meadow…

*Little ducks, soup and sheep, sunshine in
the trees…*

Figure 15 **From *Granpa* by John Burningham, published by Jonathan Cape**

see that Granpa is surrounded by signs of the feminine – a pram, dolls, a cuddly toy cosily tucked up under his table, and his grandchild in a nurse's outfit. And we see the reproachful look in his eyes and the little girl's vivid blush. It is probably in a multitude of brief and quickly-forgotten moments like this that gender is learned, but here such a fleeting instant in time becomes 'text' so that we can read it. But which of them is supposed to be imagining that playful sepia image of a female teddy bear making herself up in front of a mirror? This is no flashback, and it probably has nothing at all to do with Granpa's thoughts. It seems to be a piece of cultural mischief that has been authorially slipped in from outside the boundaries of the book, an ironic reminder of our contemporary uneasiness about sexuality and gender. The little girl is clearly interested in caring or mothering, a concern which surfaces again later when Granpa tells her he used to roll a hoop when he was a boy. She can accept that he was a boy, but she wants to take her understanding even further back in time: 'Were you once a baby *as well*, Granpa?' (my italics), perhaps trying to come to terms with the idea that he was once smaller than she is and in need of the kind of mothering she already gives her dolls.

Figure 16 From *Granpa* by John Burningham, published by Jonathan Cape

There is a similar ambiguity about the sepia drawing in the next opening. Since Granpa is reading the story of Noah, we might have expected a sketch of a flood here – but there is just a homely garden pond in the rain, with lilies and frogs. There is no reason to assume that this represents either Granpa's or the little girl's thoughts (though it might be the only way she can imagine a flood), and most young readers who have commented on it have assumed it was a picture of Granpa's garden pond, a kind of supplementary image to complete the full-colour illustration on the opposite page. This, too, is very different from those on the previous pages. It occupies the whole space, and its rich but sombre colours and rather square full-frontal composition, suggest a whole cultural structure viewed by a reader from some slightly formal distance. (It was Ann who said we were looking at the picture 'from across the river'; perhaps this was related to her perception that Granpa's house was the same as Mr Gumpy's.) It is a culture in which every detail is comfortable and suggests safety and continuity. The green gutters and drains, the water-butt and the weather-vane on the greenhouse, all indicate a domestic solidity in which everything is coping properly with the wet weather; and the large garden – with rake, wheelbarrow, potted shrub, and espaliered fruit-tree – the mature trees and the church in the background, reinforce this effect with hints of a traditional English suburban stability. The bedrooms are cosily bright, and the girl cautiously improvises on the dangers of floods as Granpa reads the story of Noah. The full double-spread of the two of them in the garden works in a similar way, using bright colours and a generous breadth of design to hint at the universality of play. Granpa makes the inevitable mistake ('It's not chocolate, it's strawberry,' he has to be told) and the little girl's pretending about shopkeeping, cooking and mothering is set within a context suggesting the seasonal rituals of suburban gardening. Granpa is sitting in a different armchair now – the summer one – and there are flower pots, a rake and a garden roller.[8]

Granpa represents a privileged culture quite unlike much of contemporary British life. But the book makes no assertions about its privilege, and does not devalue other ways of life. Its inspiration seems to spring from the best values of the culture it reflects. Furthermore, it demonstrates the unstable existential flux on which the stability appears to rest; middle-class suburban families are as subject as any others to proprietorial love, hurt and embarrassment, and bereavement. Playing and pretending are not eternal verities; they are culturally vulnerable to social and economic conditions. But it can be argued that they ought to be an eternal entitlement and that we should encourage a picture book tradition which celebrates them.

One particular page-opening ('That was not a nice thing to say to Granpa') has been the subject of a good deal of discussion. I have found that all readers can fill the gap here because every child knows, from experience, not from imagination, what it is like to say something hurtful to a grown-up. They have all done it themselves, and every reader I have asked about this has told me – in an exact demonstration of what it means to bring our knowledge of life to our reading – precisely what the granddaughter has said. One little girl suggested the child in the book had said 'willy'. This young reader had earlier said something which I had not heard clearly about the anatomy of teddy bears, so it seems likely that she linked the word which has upset Granpa with the earlier conversation about teddy being a little girl. In the picture, gesture and body posture are signs of immediate and transitory drama, quite unlike the previous picture with its suggestions of almost timeless permanence. One of the extraordinary characteristics of this picture book is the way it acknowledges that a consciousness of the slow continuity of the generations resides in individual and fleeting dramatic moments like this instant of mutual hurt.

Burningham devotes two openings to the seaside. In the first there is again a sepia drawing of two empty cane-bottom chairs and a table laid for tea. Is Granpa thinking ahead to 'tea at four o' clock'? Or is he recalling the teas of his childhood? Or is the little girl thinking about tea-time? There are no answers, and the same can be said about the sepia sketch in the next opening, which is a kind of pictorial inventory of all the features of a seaside stereotype: shells, footprints in the sand, castles, bucket and spade, starfish, a sand shoe, beach-ball, and a passing ship. Who is thinking these pale sepia thoughts? Sadie (when I had established that she was not talking about pigs) was sure Granpa was dreaming about his own childhood, because, she pointed out, the sticks on the sandcastles were old-fashioned clothes pegs, not lolly-sticks. There seems little doubt that the next drawing represents Granpa's nostalgic thoughts about the sporting kits of his youth, now symbolically draped with a cobweb.

Sadie and Ann did not trouble themselves with this sepia drawing at all. They seemed unaccountably fascinated and amused by Granpa's bare feet on the beach, and there was some giggling, rather forced – what adults are inclined to call 'silliness'. As they calmed down, Sadie reminded Ann with some amusement that all that laughing 'was going to be on the tape.' Then followed the misunderstanding about pigs, which I have already referred to. After this there was an exchange which, if analysed dispassionately, can only be described as bizarre – though it is the kind of talk that early years teachers experience daily.

Sadie	(*to Ann, playing teacher*) Come on, then.
Ann	(*reads, very hesitantly*) When I was a boy. . . .
Sadie	(*can be heard laughing in the background – why?*)
Ann	We. . . .
VW	(*prompts*) used. . . .
Ann	to roll. . . .
VW	(*prompts*) our wooden. . . .
Ann	hand. . . .
VW	(*corrects*) hoops. . . .
Ann	I've got one of them.
VW	Have you?
Ann	Not a wooden one, though.
VW	They're usually plastic these days.
Ann	. . . . down the street . . . (*long pause*) . . . after school.
Sadie	(*reads*) Where you once . . . (*self-corrects*) *Were* you once a baby as well, Granpa? I've had two teeth out.
Ann	I've had *seven* teeth out.
VW	Well, there *are* lots of gaps in your mouth. . . .
Sadie	No, I've got two . . . I've got . . . Look!
VW	Beautiful sight!
Ann & Sadie	(*counting their gaps*)
VW	(*trying to get back to* Granpa) Why do you think. . . .?
Sadie	These two are wobbly now.
VW	Why do you think she asks him if he was once a baby?
Sadie	I don't know. Because he's old now.
VW	Is he very old?
Ann	Yes, he's eighty.
Sadie	He's thirty-two, I think.
Ann	Thirty-*three*.
Sadie	Or a hundred, then.

Ann	Because my Dad is thirty-two, and my Mum's thirty-two.
Sadie	My Mum is forty-one and my Dad's forty.
VW	My Dad's eighty-eight.
Sadie	Well, he would be. You're. . . .
Ann	My dad's forty-two, and my Mummy's forty-two.
VW	Let's move on, shall we.
Sadie	Well, your Dad *would* be that older than you. (*Reads:*) If I catch a whale . . . ■

The easy moving in and out of the text, the effortless and untroubled shift from *Granpa* to the personal drama of lost teeth, the shameless number-bragging about teeth and parental age, the inconsequential and arbitrary suggestions about Granpa's age, and the teacher's anxiety to 'get back to the text', are all characteristic of a particular kind of classroom talk. This conversation, with its mysterious and unpredictable dynamics, its private and unknowable logic, and its shameless daftness, did not tell me much about how these two young readers responded to *Granpa* – and yet it *was* a response to it. I came slowly to realise that what Sadie and Ann said bore the same kind of relationship to what I said as the granddaughter's words to her Granpa's. The conversations in *Granpa* are no more bizarre than those between Ann, Sadie and myself. Perhaps John Burningham is particularly good at capturing this. Or perhaps a book which operates through fragments and disconnectedness is likely to generate fragmentary and disconnected discourse?

In the autumnal picture of Granpa fishing from his boat, the relationship of the sepia sketch to the full-colour picture is even more uncertain (see figure 17). It seems unlikely that it is Granpa imagining himself catching a whale; the cheerful smile on the face of the whale, and the fact that the little girl is grimly holding Granpa's legs to stop him from being pulled out of the boat, suggest that *she* is imagining this, and giving herself an important supporting role. This opening is unlike the others in that the sepia drawing exactly replicates the details of the colour picture opposite – the gate, hedge, trees and distant church are carefully placed in both. Only the cow is missing. 'Perhaps the whale has eaten the cow,' one reader wondered.

If I catch a fish we can cook it for supper.

What if you catch a whale, Granpa?

***Figure 17* From *Granpa* by John Burningham, published by Jonathan Cape**

■ **Sadie** (*of the sepia picture*) That's her imagination, I think.
  VW   This picture here? Or it could be *his* imagination.
  Sadie No, cos she said, 'What if you catch a whale, Granpa.'   ■

Sadie's readiness to quote the text to support her point was impressive, and so was her reasoning – that the whale was most likely to be imagined by the protagonist who had mentioned it. Other speculations are appropriate: the sketch is just as likely to be another example of authorial mischief, a playful disruption of the orderly scene on the opposite page, an example of the metafictional device which David Lewis calls *excess* and which might take the form of 'verbal or narrative gigantism.'[9]

The sepia drawing in the next opening is almost certainly a flashback, with Harry, Florence and the young Granpa sledging in a landscape with a horse and cart and a distant steam train. But Sadie found it harder to be sure this time.

■ **VW**   What's happening here?

  Sadie   That's her imagination. No. It was from last . . . the Christmas she's had. She's remembering it.

  VW   You don't think *he's* remembering it?

  Sadie   (*quotes*) Because 'I remember one Christmas.'

  VW   But who says that?

  Sadie   Her. Yes, because he . . . cos Granpa. . . .   ■

Ann interrupted at that point and Sadie never got a chance to sort out the muddle. But just how old is Granpa? One of the sepia boys is wearing a hat which is more characteristic of a Kate Greenaway childhood – and a similar point might be made about the aspidistra in an earlier flashback. Memory becomes entangled with history and is shaped to some extent by its learned imagery. Meanwhile, in the other half of the opening, Granpa almost slips on the ice and is given a supporting hand by the little girl, watched by two rather sinister birds (twa corbies?) on a leafless tree.

It is interesting that, when Granpa is ill, it is the child who is absent from the illustration. The old man has no pipe, his face is crumpled, and he is wearing pyjamas and dressing-gown. A sepia drawing indicates only the props of illness, and a voice like a pitiless authorial ruling announces that Granpa can't come out to play today. There are no ambiguities here; illness is always uncompromising. Sadie and Ann dealt with this point in the picture book with a mixture of merriment and seriousness quite untypical of their usual responses – but characteristic of this occasion. Were they baffled? Were they embarrassed? Were they trying to undermine each other? Were the emotional implications too much for six-year-olds? Did this account for the apparently inappropriate laughter?

■ **Sadie**   (*very seriously*) Why can't Granpa come out to play?

  VW   Why do you think?

  Ann   Because he's ill.

  Sadie   He's very ill.

  VW   How do you know he's ill?

  Sadie   Because he's got (*pointing at the items in the sepia drawing*) that, that, that, that. . . .

  VW   What is that?

  Ann   He's dying.

  Sadie   Hot water bottle. (*burst of laughter*)

VW	You think he's dying? Really?
Sadie	He's twenty-two, so how can he be dying?
VW	We don't know he's twenty-two, we. . . .
Ann	He's twenty-hundred. ■

Overleaf, the little girl invites Granpa into a pretended future while the left-hand sketch shows an imagined past, with what looks like a pre-war lake-steamer. Ann had little to say about this opening and it seems likely to me that Sadie's greater readiness to speculate is at least partly due to her having a confident possession of the concept of 'imagination'. Throughout this discussion, she had used the word 'imagine' several times, and it appears again here, though in an unusual form.

■ **Sadie**	(*reads*) Tomorrow shall we go to Africa, and you can be the captain.
Ann or Sadie?	(*another burst of laughter*)
VW	Who says that, do you think?
Sadie	Her.
VW	(*to Ann*) Do you think it's her?
Ann	(*non-committal*) Mmm.
VW	And what's that (*the sepia picture*) a picture of?
Sadie	She's imaginationing (*sic*) that. Yes, because she said that tomorrow shall we go to Africa? ■

Again, Sadie assumes an orderly connection between thought and word.

The final double-opening is a kind of intensification of the earlier illustrations – but an intensification through reduction. This opening illustrates absence. *Granpa* has throughout celebrated *presence*, the full, existential and physical reality of two people intensely present to one another. But that quality has been surrounded all along by absences: where is Grandma? Is she dead? Where are the child's parents? Now absences have invaded the little girl's life, and Granpa – and all his trappings, pipe, slippers, etc. – have been swept away. His chair is eloquently empty – and the emptiness seems to have taken possession of the little girl's body too; she has moved to the left-hand page and become a colourless sepia figure, a child in a nightie, with bare feet, crouched on a bleak wooden chair (see figure 18). Her face is almost featureless and her

Figure 18 From *Granpa*
by John Burningham,
published by Jonathan Cape

form comprises only a few unbroken lines. This triumph of minimalist draughtmanship is a depiction of bereavement.

Ann had almost nothing to say about this opening, and Sadie ranged from seriousness to clowning.

■ **VW**   What do you think has happened?
   Sadie He's died.
   VW   (*to Ann*) Do you think that's what happened?
   Ann   No. . . .
   Sadie Yes. . . .
   Ann   He's gone to put his slippers on. (*laughs*)   ■

This seems almost like a wilful misreading on Ann's part, a denial of the serious implications of the whole illustration. But it was not as mischievous as it seemed, for Ann had on other occasions drawn attention to the prominence of slippers in both John Burningham's and Anthony Browne's books. But Sadie firmly rejected this notion.

■ **Sadie** No, I think he's died.
   VW   Sadie, why do you think he has died?
   Sadie Cos he isn't in his chair like he usually was. And he's ill. And how

92

> can he get out of his chair? . . . because she's supposed to be helping him.
>
> **VW**   Does she look sad?
>
> **Sadie** She looks sad because he's died.
>
> **VW**   How do you know she's sad?
>
> **Sadie** Because I do, because I've seen. She looks *astonished* actually, because – look at her mouth, she's going (*mimes open-mouthed astonishment*). ■

I think Sadie was wrong about the little girl looking astonished. But it was another example of the way she would discover a new word and allow it to 'cue' approximate understandings. 'Astonishment' figured a lot in her talk at that time. She said that Angry Arthur was 'astonished' by the things that came out of his TV set.

Then the seriousness seemed suddenly too much for her and she clowned a mock-distress cry: 'Granpa! Where are you?' in a theatrical wavering voice. This made them both giggle, but their laughter was cut short abruptly when I turned the page to the final picture in which the girl is shown pushing a pram up a hillside (see figure 19).

Figure 19 **From *Granpa* by John Burningham, published by Jonathan Cape**

I have described elsewhere (see chapter 8) Sadie's immediate and warm-hearted response to any story involving friendship or caring. She instantly saw these qualities in the final picture, and made her reading explicit while Ann worked out the time-scale of the generations.

■ **Sadie**	(*very seriously*) Aaah!
Ann	Now she's grown up and . . . (*inaudible*) . . . a baby.
VW	Oh, you think that's what happened. How do you know she's grown up? Her hair's longer, I noticed.
Ann	And she's got a baby.
VW	Unless it's a doll's pram?
Sadie or Ann?	Yes.
Sadie	The dog's looking after her.
VW	Is that Granpa's dog? ■

– and that question took us back through the whole picture book in search of dogs.

At first sight, this final single-page colour illustration seems to offer precisely the reassurance that Ann and Sadie clearly found there. Life will go on, it seems to suggest. But it is not as simple as that, for it seems also to remind us that life *went on in the past*. We cannot be sure who the girl is; her hair is longer, she looks older, but the pram is from the 1930s. There is an air of angry energy about her as she pushes the pram uphill; her posture is one of *effort*, not at all suggestive of the comfortable unhurried 'play' that Granpa and the little girl were able to enjoy. Could this be Florence authorially remembered from the past, pushing the baby Granpa in his pram? She is followed by a dog; and there have been dogs in some of the pictures, of indeterminate character and different colours, but it is by no means certain that it is the grown-up Granpa's dog in this picture. For young readers, it is a hopeful image which looks ahead towards a recovered future. It seems also to be a looking-back towards a receding past, and – if this is so – the girl's future and the old man's past have become the same thing.

A couple of weeks later Ann and Sadie (who were pretending to be sisters that day) shared *Come away from the water, Shirley*[10] with me. To my surprise, they read it as two unrelated stories, but when we came to consider whether the left-hand pictures knew what the right-hand pictures were up to, they found it hard to agree on a satisfactory explanation of the connection.

■ **Ann** (*explaining the left-hand sequence*) They're going onto the beach, and then dad gets a bit tireder, then he gets tireder, and then gets more tireder, then he gets more tireder . . .

Sadie (*pointing*) He gets fed up there.

Ann Yes.

Sadie (*pointing at another illustration*) Fed up again.

Ann No, he's half-asleep, then he's asleep.

Sadie Then he puts his paper so he don't hear anything.

VW And all the time this is going on. . . .

Sadie Probably this is a dream.

VW Oh, so she's having this dream. . . .

Sadie No, he.

VW Well, who's in that picture? Who's that there?

Sadie Mum, dad, and she.

VW So you think he's having this dream about his daughter?

Sadie Yes.

VW What does Ann think?

Ann If . . . the little girl is in the sea, um . . . the man could dream that . . . she's in the sea.

Sadie So you're saying the same as me? ■

This short exchange demonstrates how a single word can have a decisive effect on a conversation. Sadie's perception ('Probably this is a dream') is a good one, and shows her understanding of one of the many forms of the story-within-a-story convention. The misunderstanding that followed occurred because she not unreasonably assumed that the dreamer was likely to be the sleeper. Ann hesitantly agreed, but I suspect she was not convinced. It was typical of Sadie that she wanted to clear up the uncertainty and establish whether they were in agreement. Then:

■ **VW** Who's dreaming it?

Sadie The dad.

Ann No, the little girl.

Sadie (*pointing at the mother*) No, *she's* not sleeping.

95

Figure 20 From *Come away from the water, Shirley* by John Burningham, published by Fontana

Ann	No, look. . . .
VW	Ann means the little girl, not the mummy.
	(*long thoughtful silence*)
Sadie	(*very uncertainly*) She. . . .
VW	That's the mummy, and that's the daddy, and Ann thinks the little girl herself. . . . ■

These were ordinary misunderstandings and were quickly cleared up. But Sadie was still confused about the fundamental disagreement and, in the next part of the conversation, Ann took things forward by 'correcting' the word *dream*. But that took them into an unexpected existential dilemma!

■ **Ann**	No, she isn't dreaming but she's *thinking* about it.
Sadie	Well, she's *in* the boat!
Ann	No, but she's *thinking* about she's in the boat.
Sadie	How can she when she's already in there?

Ann	Cos she's *thinking* that she's in there.
VW	I think Ann means. . . .
Sadie	(*distressed*) But she *is*!
VW	I think Ann means that she is pretending. (*long pause, and then –*)
Sadie	Yes. ■

Was this nothing more than a muddle? Or were these two six-year-olds working out a metaphysical problem? Whatever it was, I offered the word *pretending* as a further conceptual refinement. Perhaps this was an unwarranted intervention on my part, but time and my tape were running out. More importantly, Sadie's disagreement had brought her almost to tears. It is typical of her that, after a short pause for thought, she conceded without fuss. It would not have helped for me to have pointed out that this was an open text and that her reading was valid and logical. She disliked uncertainties and disagreements; Sadie was not a post-modernist reader. [11]

Many commentators agree that contemporary picture books – and especially those of John Burningham and Anthony Browne – display many of the textual features often referred to as post-modernist. However, Browne and Burningham are post-modernist in fundamentally different ways. I was led to this thought by Sadie's confusion and distress over Shirley's pretended pirate game. This was in sharp contrast with the fact that both Sadie and Ann – from when they were only four until they were almost seven – accepted the bizarre and often baffling imagery of Browne's illustrations as a matter for delight and laughter. I have a tape of them sharing *Kirsty Knows Best*[12] a book about a little girl imagining an alternative life; it is too long to analyse here, but it demonstrates their shared and uninhibited delight as they spotted the many secret pictorial jokes and intertextual ironies embedded there. It was a 'happy' reading. Sadie was *never* distressed by the evocative inconclusivenesses of Anthony Browne's picture books.

Browne's books are disorderly and comic, and young readers recognise the game and play it delightedly. But Burningham's picture books are deeply conservative and almost religiously serious, and they are mostly about order. The seriousness of *Granpa* arises from the strong authorial sense of both the disruptions and the continuities of time. The page openings shift repeatedly from the transitory to the permanent, from the dying to the lasting, and they suggest an orderliness existing in the very disruptions of daily life. When Ann observed that Granpa's house is the same as Mr Gumpy's, she was right in more ways than she probably intended: *Mr Gumpy's Outing*[13] is about an orderly life, with one brief disruption quietly anticipated and quickly set right. Perhaps all Burningham's picture books are increasingly complex poetic improvisations on a theme of Gumpiness. Certainly, beneath the fragmented and disordered surface of *Granpa* there is a strong sense of a learned and socially transmitted order of class and stability. It may not be a post-modernist text at all, for it says little about today's divided and distracted consciousness (except, perhaps, in the opening which shows them both watching TV while at least one of them is thinking about something else). In fact, it *resists* division and distraction by offering as a reassuring alternative the incomplete, inarticulate but essentially loving intercourse between adult and child.

Ann and Sadie were very different readers (see Chapters **8** and **11**) and I do not think it is possible from their experience to generalise about children reading post-modernist texts in a post-modernist age. Sadie was upset by *Come away from the water, Shirley* partly because she liked causal connections to be understood and explicitly *agreed* and also, I believe, because she recognised – especially in *Granpa* – John Burningham's seriousness and needed to answer it with her own. A serious book invites a serious reading, and a book about order invites an understanding of its coherence.

It has become almost commonplace to argue that today's young readers find themselves in a world in which consciousness has been to a significant extent changed by technology, and that they are for the most part more comfortably in sympathy with its epistemological demands than many adults. I subscribe to that view. However, in spite of the confusing post-Thatcherite video culture of marketed intertexts, that does *not* mean that children have been transformed into aliens with thought processes beyond our comprehension. They are no more inaccessible than Burningham's little girl is to Granpa. Ann had a quiet insouciance which enabled her to rest comfortably with tacit understandings; Sadie seemed to need the coherence to be endorsed by explicit agreement. Both of them in their responses to *Granpa*, showed precisely the same need as Granpa's little girl – a need for cultural coherence, for meanings made out of the hints and misunderstandings of ordinary experience.

If we analyse the utterances of the little girl in *Granpa*, we find that there are seven questions, an interest in the comparative ages of young and old, one or two bafflingly private remarks, an awareness of the failings of adults (Ann and Sadie discovered that I had forgotten to switch on the tape-recorder until halfway through the reading!) and some inconsequential daftness. An analysis of Sadie's and Ann's contributions to the discussion with me about *Granpa* shows more or less the same features, in more or less the same proportions.

> "May we come with you?" said the children.
> "Yes," said Mr Gumpy.

ACKNOWLEDGEMENT

I am grateful to the staff and pupils at Histon and Impington Infant's School, near Cambridge, for giving me regular access to the school for several years, and for allowing me to work with young readers and collect the evidence on which this chapter, and chapters 8 and 11 are based.

REFERENCES

1 John Burningham, *Granpa*. London: Jonathan Cape, 1984.

2 Jill Murphy, *Peace at Last*. London: Macmillan, 1980.

3 Pat Hutchins, *Rosie's Walk*. London: Bodley Head, 1970.

4 Shirley Hughes, *Up and Up*, London: Bodley Head, 1979.

5 David Lewis, 'The Constructedness of Texts,' *Signal 62*, May, 1990.

6 Or perhaps they already were. Perhaps all young readers of today are post-modernist? Peter Hunt believes that the complexity of *Granpa* is 'closer to the comprehension patterns of an orally based reader.' Peter Hunt, *Criticism, Theory and Children's Literature*. Oxford: Blackwell, 1991.

7 Judith Graham, *Pictures on the Page*, NATE, 1990, p. 109.

8 Garden rollers are a particularly effective symbol of suburban permanence: they are often too heavy to be taken by furniture removers and thus remain in the same garden for generations.

9 David Lewis, ibid.

10 John Burningham, *Come away from the water, Shirley* London: Fontana, 1983.

11 It has been suggested that the subject of *Granpa* is too distressing for young readers. I have never found it so – and it is worth pointing out that Sadie was upset by a conceptual difficulty she had with *Shirley*, but not at all by Burningham's picture book narrative of bereavement.

12 Annalena McAfee, illus. Anthony Browne, *Kirsty Knows Best*, London: Julia MacRae Books, 1987.

13 John Burningham, *Mr Gumpy's Outing.* London: Jonathan Cape, 1970.

Spying on picture books with young children

Helen Bromley

I can still remember the day when Helen Bromley rushed into an Inset meeting clutching dozens of pieces of children's writing and artwork. 'I have just had the most amazing day,' she announced. The results of that amazing day's work (and the days that followed) are documented in this chapter. Little of Helen's excitement has worn off in this written version and her enthusiasm is still infectious. Although she has always held strong views on the capacities of young children to read pictorial texts with insight and intelligence, even Helen Bromley was surprised at the intertextual understandings of this class of six-year-olds. And their knowledge was not just related to other texts; they also demonstrated familiarity with particular artists' styles of composition. With time for reflection and background reading, particularly on narrative painting, Helen Bromley invites the reader to share the discoveries made by her 'spies' and to observe young intellects at work. She also demonstrates how teachers can analyse classroom practice and provide a supportive context where children can show the literary and artistic interpretation of which they are capable.

' . . . Talk of court news; and we'll talk with them too,
Who loses and who wins; who's in and who's out;
And take upon us the mystery of things,
As if we were God's spies: '

King Lear: [Act 5 Scene III]

Jonathan rushed over to me, clutching a copy of *Jeremiah in The Dark Woods*. On one of the pages a line drawing shows one of the characters astride a rather snappy motorbike. He was excited by this and, pointing at the picture with the sort of animation that comes from having made a great discovery, he said 'I think he must have read *Little Rabbit Foo Foo*, Miss.'[1]

What this remark showed was that Jonathan had clearly understood the purpose of the day's activities. This was to seek out intertextual links, where authors use children's ability to 'recognise in their reading what has been in their memory for some time.'[2] Of course the links that children make for themselves will depend on exactly what is or is not in their memories. *Little Rabbit Foo Foo* was a favourite text of Jonathan's, involving a fierce rabbit driving about the countryside on a motorbike, which is why he made the assumption that Allan Ahlberg knew Little Rabbit Foo Foo as well! Jonathan's great discovery was not the only one that was made that morning. I wanted to find out whether young children could make their knowledge about intertextual links explicit. For this to be successful it was essential not only to give careful consideration to the teacher's role, but also to select the right books for the children to use.

The teacher

The children gathered together for that day's activities consisted of twenty-eight six- and seven-year-olds. They were at various stages of reading development; from those who relied heavily on known texts to rehearse their reading skills, to those who could read almost anything. My role was not to instruct the children in the nature of intertextuality and then test the success of my teaching, but rather to enable them to identify it for themselves before going off, like spies, to record its appearance in texts of their own choosing.

Janet and Allan Ahlberg are recognised as masters of the polysemic text and as their books were well known to the children, the session began by re-reading these old favourites. Some time was also spent looking closely at familiar texts by Anthony Browne and David McKee.

The discussion which followed clearly demonstrated that the children had no need for formal instruction. I started by asking them to identify the

stories and nursery rhymes that they recognised in *The Jolly Postman*[3].
Little hands shot up in the air like rockets on bonfire night. There wasn't
anyone who didn't feel part of this discussion. Having lit the blue touch-
paper, as it were, I observed how these children demonstrated not only
the knowledge that they possessed, but also how they felt about it. 'It
makes you feel really clever when you spot something from another book,'
was one comment. A little girl got right to the heart of it when she said,
'You sort of hug yourself inside.' These children were acknowledging the
conspiratorial feeling described by Margaret Meek and Frank Smith; that
process of becoming 'insiders in the network'.[4] The children showed that
they were perfectly capable of theorising their practice as readers, because
of the quality of the books they had read. The teacher's job on this
occasion, was to enable children to make their intertextual knowledge
explicit. Within the framework of conversations about books, children
can make known to us their understandings of the structures that lie
behind complex texts.

The notion of being spies appealed to the children, as I explained the
choice of activities:

1 Finding as many intertextual links as they could and recording them

The spies' mission was to spot familiar characters in stories, other than the
ones from which they originally came. As we had just discussed *The Jolly
Postman* together, I used this as a demonstration of what they had already
achieved. The idea was to repeat this activity with books of their own
choice.

2 Writing their own stories with intertextual links

The children were told they could write a story that contained characters
from other literary sources. This was not difficult for them to understand,
as children naturally use favourite TV, video, or computer game
characters in their stories as a matter of course.

3 Choosing a familiar rhyme and changing the words

I had recently explored some of Lewis Carroll's literary jokes in *Alice* with
the children. Many poetry books contain examples of parody and some of
these were read and discussed first.

4 Looking for pictorial intertextual influences of other artists' work on that of the picture book illustrators

In order to explain this task, I referred to the work that the children had done with a previous teacher. They had read *Katie's Picture Show* by James Mayhew which contains references to several famous artists whom the children learned to recognise.

5 Drawing in the style of an artist or illustrator

The children were also told that they could work singly, in pairs or in larger groups if they wished. The idea was not to ascertain each child's individual knowledge of intertextual links, but rather to facilitate the 'guided re-invention of knowledge.'[5]

The books

Using appropriate pictorial texts was clearly central to the success of the session. The children carried out their detective work in a room equipped with dozens of popular picture books. The complete works of the Ahlbergs were available to them, as were those of Anthony Browne, David McKee, John Burningham and others. One book which was particularly important to the children was *The Frog Prince Continued* by Jon Scieszka and Steve Johnson.[6] This was found by one group of 'spies' to refer not only to the fairy story of the title, but also to many other tales of that genre: Snow White, Cinderella, Hansel and Gretel etc. Indeed the humour and plot of the book is heavily reliant on the reader sharing the author's wide knowledge of fairy tales. As the beleaguered prince struggles to find a solution to his identity crisis, he seeks help from a variety of witches, each having her own particular speciality – apples (poisoned), boys (roasted), pumpkins (transformed). I watched with excitement as a group of children not only identified the intertextual links within the story, but also used the clues provided in the illustrations to divine which witch was which. The book was operating on several levels, demonstrating that the artist or story-teller can 'recruit children's imaginations.' The children identified intertextual links through pictorial as well as written clues which made the task accessible to *all* the children, whether or not they were fluent with written texts.

Spies at work

The children readily organised themselves into efficient working parties. Some chose to remain solitary, as was their right, but many worked in groups, forming excited little huddles round favourite texts, completely absorbed in the task. None of the groups merely listed the stories from other books they found. Instead they chose a combination of pictorial and written recording in the form of charts or flow diagrams. Some of these were works of art in their own right. The children were tenacious in their hunt for connections and this is evident from their drawings. Some children noted the authors' references to their own previous work; *The Jolly Christmas Postman* containing references to *The Jolly Postman* for example.

As Margaret Meek has taught us, the meanings that we make from texts depend on our previous experiences and each reader will bring something of themselves to the reading of a text. Matthew brought his chart about *Each Peach Pear Plum* [7] with Rock a Bye Baby carefully cited as one of the intertextual links. The actual reference in the text is to Baby Bunting but it transpired that this rhyme was unknown to him. He had, however used a rhyme he did know to support his construction of meaning. Matthew might not have read the rhyme Baby Bunting himself in order to recognise it in an unfamiliar context. He might have had it sung to him, heard it on a tape, seen it on a video or watched it on television. We need to remember that for many children today, media texts are the dominant texts that they encounter before school.

The intertextual links discovered by the children were not just those of a literary nature. One group of children discovered that Elmer (the patchwork elephant) was to be found on the toy shelves of the badly behaved Bernard of *Not Now Bernard* fame. This led to children making their own rules and generalisations about the styles of authors and illustrators. David McKee books were gathered together and searched for examples of patchwork. The children's tenacity was amply rewarded – the patchwork sided house in *Toucan Toucan* and the patchwork elephant pulled up the hill in *The Hill and The Rock*. There was high level cognitive activity going on here.

After the children had been shown Tenniel's illustrations for *Alice in Wonderland*, I explained to them that his source for the Duchess was the

105

painting 'A Grotesque Old Woman' and showed them a postcard of the painting from the National Gallery. They were quick to take this on board because of their knowledge of famous artists gained from an earlier project. With a little help they were able to identify Magritte and Van Gogh in *Through the Magic Mirror* and *Changes*. One boy could see the connection between Turner's paintings and John Burningham's illustrations for *Oi! Get Off Our Train!* (Various paintings by Turner had been on display in the school for some time.)

It was obvious from watching the children at work that they were emotionally engaged and intellectually challenged by the texts they were studying so closely. I believe they were attempting to share the context of authorship with the people who had created the 'possible worlds' in front of them. The context shared was a mental one; the opportunity to 'think like the author' and identify the techniques which made these narratives so intriguing. To these children, so engrossed in their collecting of evidence that day, there was far more to intertextuality than finding other stories in stories or 'getting the joke'. They were closely examining irony, parody, satire and ambiguity – the fact that words can mean so much more than they actually say. Recognising and rehearsing these techniques within the safe confines of a picture book may enable children to deal with advertisements, news reports and political propaganda with discernment at a later stage.

One task which excited the children's interest was the opportunity to draw in the style of a picture book illustrator. They had a working knowledge of artists such as Monet, Turner and Van Gogh. They knew of Magritte's influence on Anthony Browne and that the interior design of Joseph Kay's bedroom owed more to Van Gogh than to Coloural! (This may surprise some teachers, but children today are visually sophisticated and don't find it difficult to recognise the styles of different artists and do find it interesting.) What surprised me was the apparent ease with which the children could draw in the style of different artists. Christina drew a bridge over a stream mimicking Monet; Thomas drew a Turneresque sunset; and budding Anthony Brownes abounded. Behind Madeleine's castle windows lurked sunshine and rain, clouds and rainbows instead of the expected furniture and knights! She had noted Browne's skill at making the ordinary extraordinary. Another drew a pirate ship where the masts were bananas, and jungle creatures, instead of pirates, peered out from the portholes. The children had managed to extract the essential features from their chosen artist's work and combined them with an original composition of their own. Decision making is involved here, as is composition, drafting and a high level of abstract thought. The effective juxtaposition of two artistic styles clearly demonstrated the extensive knowledge that they had about the construction of a pictorial text. The children were themselves able to be authors of polysemic texts.

Some educationists have questioned whether reading too many picture books could hinder children's ability to use their own imagination. I do not believe this to be so. In order to draw their own pictures children often visualise them first. The fact that young children can identify illustrative references, as well as literary ones, is an important revelation. I think that children use illustrations as the structure on which to practise their skills of interpretation. The pictures provide a framework through which they formulate and test out hypotheses, but this does not restrict their ability to conjure up pictures in their own minds.

The skills used by the best creators of picture books are similar to those used by some of the great narrative painters. Anabel Thomas [8] suggests that 'a narrative painting can only be fully enjoyed if the story it tells is understood.' This is also true of polysemic texts. As we have seen, the more knowledge that a reader can bring to a text, the more meanings they can make from it. Anabel Thomas describes five such techniques in *The Illustrated Dictionary of Narrative Painting*. I have redescribed them in terms of picture books and how they facilitate learning outcomes. All the quotes which follow come from this book.

1 **'The painter may, like the strip cartoonist, present a number of images or stills.'**

The strip cartoon technique is found most often in wordless picture books like Jan Ormerod's *Sunshine* and *Moonlight*. In Shirley Hughes' *Up and Up*, it is used to stunning effect in the story of the little girl with the strong desire to fly. The intertextual links within this book lie not merely in identifying the sub-plots which accompany the main story; readers get more out of *Up and Up* if they know the story of Icarus and are familiar with comic strip conventions.

2 'A second technique is that of the trigger image. Painters have often used trigger images – to trigger a response to the whole narrative.'

Patchwork (David McKee) and gorillas (Anthony Browne) are trigger images, signs and symbols which children use to identify different authors and recognise familiar friends. If we expand the notion of intertextuality to intercontextual links, and think about adults' experiences as well as childrens, we might come closer to understanding the way in which polysemic texts work. When reading *Each Peach Pear Plum*, a child may recognise Baby Bunting and remember the nursery rhyme, but I would suggest that a whole lot more is being remembered as well, though not, perhaps, consciously. As an adult reader, I enjoy the rhymes, and recall the contexts in which they were read to me. Images of a comfortable, far off childhood are what these images trigger for me and, as such, contribute to enjoyable re-readings of the text.

Closely linked to the trigger image is the use of icons. Iconography is the technique where 'signs, symbols and colour are employed to identify individual figures and situations.' Thus, children begin to expect a shaggy looking dog in the books of John Burningham or the sort of world where lampposts can terrify you in the books of Satoshi Kitamura. Identifying these icons encourages children to construct and test hypotheses. For Jonathan the picture of a motorbike was synonymous with the presence of Little Rabbit Foo Foo.

3 'A third technique . . . is the introduction of circumstantial detail . . . These details of course cannot carry the story on their own but often play an important supporting role.'

Each Peach Pear Plum is an example of a book where circumstantial detail is used to great effect. Children's eyes carefully scan each page, looking for clues in the scenery. Great pleasure can be gained from scanning the frontispiece, trying to identify the owner of the washing on the line, or feeling pleased when you realise that peaches plums and pears grow in the tiny orchard outside the picturesque cottage. Is that Robin Hood's wood? Whose sheep are those? Of course, if one returns to the metaphor of spies, this is circumstantial evidence which Anthony Browne also uses to great effect. The reader is encouraged to re-read the text many times because the pictures are full of the extraordinary. The garden of the house in *The Visitors Who Came To Stay*, for example, has an egg plant, a crab-apple tree and a shoe-tree, visual jokes which evoke the outside world. The background to the pictures in *Bear Hunt* provides the same sort of reader satisfaction; plants with lips, and foliage that looks as if it has just paid a visit to the menswear department of a chain store!

It is this sort of circumstantial detail which draws the children back to the picture books over and over again. The pictures seem to be constructed so that the children will not notice every detail at first reading but will go back time and time again, working out new connections and reaffirming knowledge previously gained. After one or two readings of *Knock Knock Who's There?* the children discovered that the circumstantial detail on the wallpaper of the little girl's bedroom gave clues as to who was going to appear next at her bedroom door.

4 **'The expression of the emotion engendered by a story is a fourth way in which a painting can convey the essence of narrative. Light and colour may be crucial.'**

Catching the mood of a story through the colours of the illustrations may not seem as good an example of intertextuality as delighting in the presence of well-known characters in the Ahlbergs' books. However, I would say that it is a different sort of intertextuality: the link being with the children's lives and emotions outside the book that they are reading. I asked one group of children how they knew that dark colours were scary or sad (after they had identified them as such). The answers were very revealing. Almost everyone used a video to connect darkness with morbidity, as well as talking about fear of the dark. Children are successful at reading the pictures that use colour to depict such emotions, because they bring to the reading the context of such experiences.

The use of light and colour is particularly obvious in Anthony Browne's *Gorilla*, where quite young children can point out the difference in the lighting of scenes, reflecting the changes of mood of the characters in the story. *The Frog Prince Continued* also uses the fact that dark colours are synonymous with gloom and despondency on its opening page, leaving the reader in no doubt as to the state of the protagonists' marriage.

5 **'The last technique . . . concerns the use of facial expression and bodily gesture . . . the expression of emotion; the indication of direction and movement and a suggestion of the relationships between the characters and other features shown.'**

The power of gesture is used to great effect by picture book artists. Children asked how they know that the Frog Prince and his wife are unhappy answer with such remarks as 'they're not looking at each other', 'they look sad', 'if they were happy they would be smiling.' These remarks show how important body language is in supporting the meanings that readers make from texts.

This is particularly true when children are trying to determine the relationship of one character to another. Because we are discussing stories here this is very important. A picture of a solitary figure in a particular pose could not readily support the abstraction of meanings unless it is involved in the wider context of a story. An excellent example of this can be seen in *Granpa* by John Burningham[9], on the page which says 'That was not a nice thing to say to Granpa.' As Judith Graham points out, one can only speculate about what was said, but the effect on both the characters can be determined by the fact that they have both been illustrated.[10] Showing only one of them would not have been sufficient to create the mood. Not only do they have their backs to each other, but a large expanse of white page lies between them, emphasising the enormity of the situation. Intertextual links can be made with the context in which the child has been brought up. Shirley Brice Heath mentions the importance that adults place on gesture and body language when trying to understand the meanings made by their children. 'Children often give such (non-verbal clues), imitating or describing noises or non-verbal features that took place in connection with the object or event they are trying to use as a topic.'[11] No wonder then that they are so adept at taking meanings from picture books that use precisely those devices.

The Renaissance theorist Leon Alberti argued that body language was one of the key elements to understanding a story. 'We weep with the weeping, laugh with the laughing, and grieve with the grieving. These movements of the soul are made by movements of the body.'[12] Again this is true of the picture books. Children use their reading of pictures to support their reading of the text. There are also many instances where the pictures say far more than words ever can. It is the pictures in *The Frog Prince Continued* which supply the reader with clues as to the possible identity of the witches, and in *Each Peach Pear Plum* it is the ability to interpret gestures and facial expression that enables the reader to follow the sequence of events which leads to Baby Bunting's trip down the river. It would be interesting to ask a variety of readers which particular clue they see first. Is it the shocked face of the little rabbit (part of the circumstantial detail), the way that baby bear is drawn (body language indicating that he has fallen) or the broken rope? It is certainly not in the text which simply says 'Three bears out hunting, I spy Baby Bunting.' The face of the rabbit suggests that the bears themselves are unaware of the unfortunate incident. What the Ahlbergs have done so cleverly is to draw attention to Baby Bunting by encouraging the reader to look for him, but without telling the reader to do so or giving away the whole story.

There is no doubt in my mind that young children can successfully identify intertextual links of both a written and illustrative nature. As 'spies' they were extremely successful. Their methods of working and their ability to make their discoveries explicit were a revelation to me. It was interesting to learn that picture-book illustrators are using devices which have been around for many centuries in narrative painting. The experience underlined for me the sophistication of children today who bring to school vast experience of reading visual texts. These are skills which, as teachers, we ignore at our peril. If we work with the grain, building on children's skills and knowledge, then we too will be able to 'take upon us' the mysteries that are the literacies of the future.

REFERENCES

1 Michael Rosen, *Little Rabbit Foo Foo*. London: Walker Books, 1990.

2 Margaret Meek, *How Texts Teach What Readers Learn*. Stroud: Thimble Press, 1988.

3 Allan and Janet Ahlberg, *The Jolly Postman*. London: Heinemann, 1986.

4 Meek, 1988, op. cit.

5 Gorden Wells, *The Meaning Makers*. London: Hodder & Stoughton, 1986.

6 Jon Scieszka and Steve Johnson, *The Frog Prince Continued*. London: Viking 1991.

7 Allan and Janet, Ahlberg, *Each Peach Pear Plum*. London: Kestrel 1978.

8 Anabel Thomas, *The Illustrated Dictionary of Narrative Painting*. London: John Murray in association with the National Gallery, 1994.

9 John Burningham, *Granpa*. London: Jonathan Cape, 1984.

10 Judith Graham, Pictures on the Page, Sheffield: NATE, 1990.

11 Shirley Brice Heath, *Ways With Words*. Cambridge: Cambridge University Press, 1983.

12 Leon Alberti, in Anabel Thomas, 1994, op. cit. pp. xii.

8

Her family's voices – one young reader tuning into reading

Victor Watson

In a further encounter with the two little girls, who feature in an earlier chapter and with whom Victor Watson read books on a weekly basis for several years, we are given several snapshots of how one child in particular (Sadie) developed into an independent reader. We get a chance to observe the idiosyncratic moves towards becoming an experienced reader made by a child whose progress seems to be working in harmony with her sense of voice or voices – her family's in particular. And this engagement with text is illustrated through Sadie's reading of Satoshi Kitamura, Anthony Browne, John Burningham and Posie Simmonds, four of the most powerful picture book artists of the late twentieth century.

When I first met Sadie she was four-and-a-half. Like most of the reception readers I worked with, Sadie had great difficulty at first in sequencing stories she had heard. Invited to tell me about *Sleeping Beauty*, for example, she told me there was a witch, that the witch changed the princess into a frog, that a prince married Sleeping Beauty, and that the story ended with the witch making friends with Sleeping Beauty. Sadie was apparently not yet able to sequence the incidents of the story, or distinguish one narrative from another. She had some sense of how books 'work' – she knew about directionality, titles, illustrations, and some of the conventions of story, but the only word she recognised was her name. Her understanding was insufficient to enable her to find ways of structuring, retaining and interpreting sequenced narratives. She could not yet string the narrative beads together but she appreciated their colour and appeal. From the perspective of such young learners, the syntax of narrative must seem a kaleidoscope of shifting brightness and colour.

Sadie is a cheerful, sensible and kindly girl. She likes people. She quickly came to enjoy her shared reading sessions with me. Perhaps she was a little possessive, too, for when we were joined by her friend Ann, the dynamics were different. Sadie retained her good humour, but was not above subverting her friend's passionate excitement about pictures (see Chapter 6). Perhaps she intuitively realised that I was interested in Ann's perceptions and felt as if she were the outsider, the one who did not see so subtly into illustrations. Ann had a habit of stammering when she was excited – a weird little gasping as if she hadn't enough breath to get her words out fast enough. On my tapes of some of these three-way reading sessions, Sadie can clearly be heard quietly but determinedly imitating her friend's stammer, and this mimicry was a sure signal that Sadie was subverting the seriousness with which Ann analysed the pictures. But most of the time she was cheerfully prepared to go along with it, even when Ann corrected her quite bossily.

In the three-way discussion on *The Tunnel*[1] which occurred when both children were around four-and-a-half (see Chapter 6), Sadie made fewer unsolicited comments than Ann, and most of them were simple descriptions of something happening in the illustrations ('I think that he's left the ball behind'). This short extract from the transcript demonstrates Sadie's straightforwardly literal approach. I asked them if they had noticed anything about the sky in the sequence of four framed illustrations (see figure 21) showing Rose in a gradually transforming landscape of brightening colour. At first they both said 'No' and then, typically, it was Ann who made the first observation.

■ **Ann**   Oh, yes. That's a little bit dark and that's a bit dark. That's nearly blue and that's clear sky.

   VW   And, Sadie, you could do the same thing if you think about the grass.   ■

Prompted in this shameless manner[2] by me, Sadie did her duty.

■ **Sadie**   That's sort of a darker colour, and that's sort of a little bit darken, that is, and that's light.   ■

In making these observations she sounded a little half-hearted, as if she

113

Figure 21 From *The Tunnel* by Anthony Browne, published by Julia MacRae Books

was doing her best to imitate her friend in order to play a game without knowing why it mattered. But there was nothing half-hearted in Ann's next contribution; she had noticed something else in the illustrations.

■ **Ann**   I can say the difference of those.
VW   Well, I would like you to.
Ann   They're all stones, and those you can't really see and those bits you can't a bit see, and they're just flowers you *can* see.   ■

Earlier, Ann had explained that the brother came back to life because his sister cuddled him. The warming from stone to life is also suggested here by the way Anthony Browne allows the small ring of stones to become gradually transformed into daisies. It was the kind of symbolic use of image that I knew Ann was excited by, and so I asked about it.

■ **VW**   How did they turn into daisies?
Sadie   Because they just growed into flowers.
Ann   No. Because he's a stone first and then they come . . . they come . . . . to . . . (*inaudible stammering*). . . .
Sadie   The flowers started to grow!
Ann   The flowers started to grow.   ■

Sadie's first emphatically literal explanation was not enough for Ann and her reference to the boy ('he's a stone first') shows that she was trying to find words to explain the symbolism, to link the stone flowers with the stone boy, and the ultimately with Anthony Browne's theme of love restoring life. But her stammering tentativeness was too much for Sadie, who offered her own less complicated explanation. Her tone of voice was not dismissive or impatient, just kindly and good-humoured, like an elder sister affectionately tolerant of the younger child's odd fussing. Ann (the youngest and smallest child in the school at that time) was probably tired by then and gave up, gratefully accepting the simpler suggestion.

There was a similar exchange at the end of the discussion, when Ann explained to Sadie why the brother's ball and the sister's book are side-by-side in the final endpaper (see pages 148–9). It was a long and not very clear account, and when I asked Sadie if she agreed with it, she replied simply 'Yep!' It was an eloquent monosyllable, cheerful, polite, but final. [3]

115

She couldn't see what the fuss was about but was willing to go along with it and keep us both happy.

When I played back these tapes at a later date, I realised that I had failed to appreciate what some would call Sadie's 'social skills'. I dislike the expression. It suggests a cerebral and manipulative rule-learning, and it does not do justice to the unobtrusive personal tact Sadie showed in her dealings with other people. She did not develop a set of 'tact skills', they were Sadie herself – kind, sensitive, fascinated by people, good-humoured, and not above the occasional touch of mischief.

Sadie learnt fast. Her work with the classteacher was giving her a confident awareness of common phonic correspondences and she could be seen trying out the sounds of initial consonants. She had a less sure grasp of vowels, but this was rarely a problem becase she was developing a wide sight-vocabulary, and she was doing a good deal of varied writing. When she was alone with me, she preferred texts with repetitions or refrains (*The Enormous Turnip, Knock, Knock, Who's There?, Mr Gumpy's Outing*[4]) and we always negotiated how we would share the reading. Either we took parts or we read alternate pages, and sometimes when she was tired I read all the words and she talked about the pictures. She repeatedly chose her favourites until she knew them so well that she was clearly 'half-reciting, half-deciphering'[5] them, and her growing confidence in phonic awareness was a support. However, despite this evident progress, there was a mechanical quality in her reading, a businesslike and determined code-breaking approach to something she knew she had to learn. Where there was humour in a story, she sometimes had a slightly baffled look. I believe her enjoyment was a social one; she liked going to the school library to read with me, and she enjoyed the books – but reading the actual words was not yet part of the pleasure. I have no way of being certain about this, but the indications were that Sadie was developing into a competent independent reader but with little interest in the process.

Then there was a change. It became apparent to me when she was six-and-a-half and we were reading *The Tunnel*[6] again which she had not seen since she had shared it with Ann two years earlier. Sadie was clearly reading for meaning now. There were few prompts, and there was a lot of talk about the illustrations. Mostly she asked questions ('What's that?')

and there were gasps and slightly comical shudders when she looked at the illustrations of the forest. She had a good understanding of how pictures work; when I asked her why there was a smear of red behind Rose's coat, she said (patronisingly, as if I really should have known), 'That makes the *speed*.'

But what took me by surprise was that she self-corrected not for misread words (there weren't many) but when she got the intonation wrong. She had an ear for family conversations. 'Their mother grew impatient with them,' she read faultlessly, and went on to capture brilliantly the expression of the mother's voice in the dialogue. And when she volunteered her own comments on the illustrations, she spoke in the same maternal voice, confidently adopting the role of an exasperated adult remarking on the behaviour of tiresome children. There was probably some gendered behaviour here, but she read all the dialogue with great expression, including the brother's dismissive 'Don't be so *wet*.' 'Oh, dear!' she said grimly, as Rose entered the tunnel – and this was partly a narrative prediction but also a wise adult's anticipation of child-trouble. When we turned to the first forest picture she gave an audible (but untranscribable) shudder of not unpleasant horror.

This interest in voice and tone seemed a new phenomenon, but later I came to realise that she had been developing this learning all the time. She was interested in people and their stories, and attentive to their voices. Most of all she had learned the 'tunes' of family talk. Perhaps those code-breaking skills she had been diligently but rather drearily acquiring now made possible an unknown moment of discovery, and when Sadie found these tunes in the books she read, she discovered a new sense of recognition and power.

It is not enough to say that Sadie was 'reading with expression'. Such bland phrasing gives no sense of the extraordinary and transforming effect on her of having found her voices – her family's voices taken over and made into her own. This power of creative ventriloquism gave her a perspective, an imaginative stance that provided her with a readerly approach to stories. It was as if she now knew *why* stories were interesting. She still disliked mysteries and loose ends, and so she preferred to find reasons for the gaps and mysteries in *The Tunnel*: she explained the tree

117

stumps and various other puzzles by suggesting that a witch (although there aren't any witches in the story) did these 'bad things'. But when she was not working out causal links, she filled the gaps with a kind of adult half-playful dismay expressed in grown-up phrasing and intonation. I could hear the voices of Sadie's family being subtly ventriloquised.

At about this time Sadie chose *Angry Arthur*[7] from my box. This was when I first realised the power of her new 'conversational facility.' Kitamura's words were in fact quite difficult for her, and she needed a few more promptings than usual. [8] But the nature of the story spoke directly to Sadie: the narrative invited expressions of dismay, disapproval and surprise. I wish there was a way of transcribing from the tape the confidently adult intonations of her utterances, the ease with which she 'sang' the parental tunes, her sense of the drama of the narrative.

– 'Where are the people gonna *live*?'
– 'Oh, *God*!'

And the repeated 'But it wasn't' she said in an adult and knowing way, with her eyebrows playfully raised. I tried to explain 'universequake' but she was not interested. What interested and amused her was the naughtiness, the practical consequences, the involvement of the members of Arthur's family. We talked about the illustrations in some detail. Sadie often asking questions about them and then answering herself. 'I don't like the look of *that*!' she remarked once, but mostly she loved their absurdity.

■ **Sadie**	That's coming out of the TV!	
VW	It is, isn't it?	
Sadie	He's . . . er . . .	
VW	He's what?	
Sadie	He's astonished. [9]	
VW	He . . . Well, wouldn't you be astonished if a little waggon and a cactus and arrows came out of your TV set?	
Sadie	(*laughs*)	■

(I should point out that at about this time, Sadie discovered the word 'astonished' and used it repeatedly. It seemed to make possible for her a whole new range of understandings.)

In this reading, the voices of her own family – probably, for the most part her mother – 'met' the situation in the narrative. At one point, this 'meeting' became explicit when Sadie linked Arthur's story with her own. After one of the references to Arthur's anger:

■ **Sadie**   That's what I do.
  VW   Do you?
  Sadie   Yes, and afterwards I have to go up to bed, and then Daddy comes up and says, 'You can watch TV if you like.'
  VW   Oh, I see . . .
  Sadie   And Mummy comes up and says, 'What's she doing in *our* bed?'   ■

This was a personal anecdote prompted by the story, but it also demonstrated Sadie's ability to 'sing' her parent's voices. Her subtle intonation made her father sound a grudging but affectionate softie, and she managed to suggest that her mother was no longer angry but still grumpy. Kitamura's story met Sadie's story, and her words met his. Her anecdote represented her mother and father and herself as reassuringly *comic* and enabled her to adopt a comfortable spectatorial role towards them.

Sadie's new-found conversational confidence sometimes expressed itself in a precisely appropriate exclamation. Once, when Ann and Sadie were sharing *Kirsty Knows Best* [9], at the picture of Kirsty's mother singing cabaret at a nightclub, Ann commented 'That's Kirsty's mother.' That was a literal and exact recognition. But Sadie's reaction was a simple but eloquent exclamation 'Phew!' (The tape is not clear; it might have been 'Strewth!')

The Chocolate Wedding [10] was a particularly good choice for Sadie. We had already shared *Lulu and the Flying Babies* [11], and she asked, very concisely: 'How come she does *two* Lulus?' And a little later she noticed that the brother is bigger in this story than he was in the first, and concluded that they were all a little older. *The Chocolate Wedding* is a family story with a little girl at centre-stage, and adults reacting in various ways to naughtiness, sickness and muddle. Because the text is composed very largely of speech-bubble talk, Sadie found plenty of opportunities to 'do the voices'. She interjected fewer comments as she read, possibly because

119

the kinds of exclamation she liked to make were already built into the story.

The Chocolate Wedding is not an easy text, and I sensed that Sadie was tired.

■ **VW**   Shall I read a bit, or do you want to go on?
 Sadie   (*a little on her dignity*) I think I will go on.   ■

I was impressed by her determination, which probably had something to do with the fact that there was a lot in the character of Lulu that Sadie recognised and responded to. She was willing to work patiently at some quite difficult words, syllabically working out, for example, 'petticoats' and 'strawberry'. To attack unfamiliar vocabulary like this, and at the same time to read with her usual authentic and varied intonation – a kind of 'role-play reading' – was a demanding task. Significantly, she interrupted the reading to tell me about a wedding she had been to, demonstrating the way such 'homely' stories admit the reader into the narrative. Perhaps another way of putting it is to say that the narrative is admitted into the reader's life.

(a)   **(b)**

Figure 22 Two little girls – the first one (*a*) taken from *Granpa* and the
      second (*b*) from *Aldo*, both by John Burningham, published by
      Jonathan Cape

She enjoys stories in which one character supports another [12] – and that, too, probably reflects the quality of her family life. When she read *Aldo* [13] she was more thoughtfully subdued than usual. She limited herself to reading the words, and I found myself reverting to my old way of asking about the illustrations. Once she told me firmly I would have to wait and see. She read in a rather sober voice, perhaps responding to the darker tones of this story. She said nothing about loneliness, but on several occasions she interjected a thoughtful 'Ah!' when Aldo did something particularly kind for the girl in the story. Only once did she make this explicit 'He's very kind,' she said. *Aldo* did not invite into play Sadie's family's voices, but it did reveal her interest in caring and kindness, and probably her unspoken understanding of loneliness. Perhaps it was the idea of loneliness or sadness that prompted her to suggest that this little girl was the same as the one in Burningham's *Granpa* [14], (see figure 22) an observation which indicated not just an understanding of intertext, but an intuitive grasp of Burningham's ability to deal with private feelings that lie too deep for words. While Anthony Browne's picture books allow all readers to enter his narratives on almost equal terms, blurring the distinction between the apprentice and the skilled reader, John Burningham speaks to the privacy of each reader.

Sadie came to be in confident possession of her family's voices, and this in time had a great deal to do with her becoming a reader. In fact, it was probably a two-way process, in which the reading also confirmed the value of the family talk. In such a situation, reading becomes a matter both of recognition and participation: Sadie was addressing the wider world, talking from her culture, to her culture, and about her culture.

But how were her family's voices admitted into the reading process? Almost certainly, it had a lot to do with the manner and theme of the books available. Stories about recognisable family situations, or with a great deal of family talk, or which invited laughter, authenticated Sadie's own vernacular, and took reading beyond the necessary building-up of phonic skills and banks of sight-words. It may also have something to do with an apprenticeship approach which sees reading partly as community and conversation, a collaborative, reassuring and exploratory enterprise which respects and empowers the sharing of meaning; a kind of talk, in fact.

REFERENCES

1 Anthony Browne, *The Tunnel*. London: Julia MacRae Books, 1989.

2 Transcribing my tapes brought home to me the fact that I make many interventions, some of which might be described as intrusive. I am unapologetic about this, since the tapes also show that – in the extended 'reading friendship' that developed over two years – the children were blithely capable of disregarding my interventions, and frequently adopted an adult's voice to put me right about some matter of importance.

3 Two years later, Sadie explained the daisies quite differently: she linked the fact that the girl in the story is named after a flower – Rose.

4 Mary Shepherd, *The Enormous Turnip*. London and Glasgow: Collins Educational, 1989; Sally Grindley, illus. Anthony Browne, *Knock, Knock, Who's There?* London: Hamish Hamilton, 1985; John Burningham, *Mr Gumpy's Outing*. London: Jonathan Cape, 1970.

5 Jean-Paul Sartres, *Les Mots*. Paris: Éditions Gallimard, 1964, p. 36.

6 Anthony Browne, op. cit.

7 Satoshi Kitamura, *Angry Arthur*. London: Anderson Press, 1982.

8 Sadie liked saying 'Satoshi Kitamura' over and over, as if it were an enjoyable tongue-twister, or a mantra. One day she spread out all the Kitamura books I had on the table so that she could compare them.

9 Annalena McAfee, illus. Anthony Browne, *Kirsty Knows Best*. London: Julia MacRae Books, 1987.

10 Posy Simmonds, *The Chocolate Wedding*. London: Jonathan Cape, 1990.

11 Posy Simmonds, *Lulu and the Flying Babies*. London: Jonathan Cape, 1988.

12 This was the occasion when Sadie told me she was almost a proper reader but was pleased that I would always be there to help her. That was my last visit to her school but she did not know that.

13 John Burningham, *Aldo*. London: Jonathan Cape, 1991.

14 John Burningham, *Granpa*. London: Jonathan Cape, 1984.

9

Reading *The Beano*: A young boy's experience

Michael Rosen

Michael Rosen provides a personal, yet scholarly, account of the serious attention his son, Isaac, aged six, bestows on comics. Critics have recently begun to recognise the higher order reading skills which operate within comic conventions and Michael Rosen illustrates some of these possibilities through observations of, and discussion with, one particular young reader. Isaac exemplifies the usual characteristics in his addiction to *The Beano*: a wide knowledge of numerous weekly back-issues; total absorbtion in this literacy event; the ability to read between the lines; understanding of the role of comedy in written and pictorial text, and much, much more. Michael Rosen is alert to what the reader brings to the text and lays out for us the complex range of skills which Isaac exhibits with such ease because he is, of course, engaged in self-chosen, pleasurable reading. It would be hard to dismiss comics as trivial after reading this chapter.

How we become readers is usually and conventionally discussed in relation to children's books and/or reading schemes. Yet, it is clear from observation that children set about informing themselves about reading in a wide variety of situations. One key phase is the process of learning *what reading is for*, what it can do for you. I noticed with my youngest child, Isaac, that for a period of some six months or so he became obsessive about *The Beano*. It seemed to be an obsession beyond enjoying the jokes. I was fairly sure at the time that this phase was a vital and necessary part of how Isaac was going to become a reader. I thought that one way I could find out more of what was going on would be to interview him.

It was three weeks before his sixth birthday (May 28 1993) and we talked about the issue of May 22 1993. Isaac would get every issue as it came out, but would also read back copies. Every morning, but especially at the weekends, he would get up, go downstairs, and get out the two baskets of past issues of *The Beano* and sit on the floor in a praying position, propped up on his arms leaning over a copy of the comic that lay on the floor in front of him. He did this in the entrance to the kitchen, so that we had to step over him in order to get to the kitchen. While he read, he would make no sound, no laughter, no 'listen to this', no reading out loud. These reading sessions would last up to an hour, in which time, he would have read maybe as many as thirty or forty issues. By the age of six-and-a-half he knew virtually every copy of *The Beano* that had come out in the previous three years.

By interviewing Isaac, I was hoping to find out how he read the comic. So I asked him the following kinds of questions:

1 Generic, for example, '*What is a comic?*'

2 Formalistic, for example, '*Who is speaking?*'

3 Reader-situational for example, '*When do you read? Do you talk to school-friends about* The Beano?'

4 Structural, for example, '*Are these all about naughty boys who get caught?*'

5 Ideological, for example, '*What's the moral?*'

6 Reader-responsive, for example, '*Why is this funny? Why is it your favourite?*'

7 Narrative competence/repertoire/intertextuality, for example, '*How do you know it's not true?*'

Genre

As adults, we might want to categorise *The Beano* as a form of literature distinguishable from most books in visual terms with its use of the strip; in content terms with its multi-story elements and its continuing series of narratives around the same characters; and in publication terms with its regular appearance in weekly intervals. We notice that *The Beano*

announces itself with a front page headline in blue and red on yellow: 'THE
UK's No. 1 COMIC' *The Beano*, 1993 p. 1). This follows a pattern which can
be found right across literature – the item announcing its own genre on
the cover, for example, 'A great new thriller/romance/classic/play' etc.

I asked Isaac what he thought that announcement meant and he had no
idea. He did not know what the UK was. He was, however, fairly certain
what a comic was, 'It's something you read like a book, always in paper.'
So I said, 'What's the difference between a book and a comic then?' and
he said that books can be paperback or hardback but 'comics are never
hardback'. He then said, 'There are different pages for different things.
There are pages named after characters.' I found this interesting, in that
even with a hint ('What about the pictures?') he did not isolate any
graphic aspect of comics as genre-specific. Perhaps this is a reflection on
the development of children's picture books. One of his favourite authors
is Posy Simmonds and a book like *Fred* which tells its story in a strip
format. Picture books are no longer totally distinguishable from comics in
terms of graphics. For Isaac, what is important is the *structure* of a comic,
with its sequence of subjects which relate back to previous issues rather
than with each other.

I asked Isaac who he thought wrote *The Beano* and he said, 'Dunno, it
doesn't say.' The implication here is that he knows that virtually all the
books he reads do 'say' who has written them. So I asked him *where* did
he think it was written and he said, 'Do you know *Press Gang*?' [A TV
series set in a teenage newspaper office]. I said I did. 'I think they do it in
a room like that. A work room.' In terms of reading sophistication, this is
quite significant. It means that by six, this particular child knows that a
comic does not simply appear, but is made in an office somewhere. I then
asked him if he thought one person made it and he answered with a
question, 'What's an editor?' I said it was someone who made sure that
everything was done to get the magazine or comic finished so that it
looked right and there weren't any mistakes. But why had Issac asked the
question? He said, 'Because sometimes you hear the editor's voice.' In
other words he had noticed that the cartoonist had introduced a caption
with the word 'editor' in it. He then recounted how in one instalment of
'The Bash Street Kids' there was an 'Editor's note' which said 'something
about not letting us see Olive's food being eaten.'

So here Isaac is not quite *au fait* with the idea of an editor, even though there is one in *Press Gang*. The parodied intervention by 'Editor' as in *Private Eye* is missed by him. However, it is interesting that his question about who is the editor was unsolicited and the joke does not appear in the particular issue of *The Beano* that we were looking at together. In other words, *The Beano* (and we shall see this elsewhere) initiates its readers into various kinds of graphic, intertextual and parodic jokes that its readers have to learn. Isaac is at a stage, perhaps no different from a wide range of readers, where he is initiated in some but not in others. Thus, we have here a complication of the word 'reading'. Isaac 'reads' the words, 'Editor's note' because he can transliterate these English words, but he can't 'read' (understand) the joke. When I had told him what an editor was, he probably grasped something of the idea but at this time did not yet realise the nature of the parody of the blue-pencil-in-hand editor, subbing dubious copy and discreetly protecting his readers from sordid scenes. Reading *The Beano* is not quite as simple as it seems . . .

Formalistic

This leads us into a formalistic question – Who speaks in *The Beano*? Isaac said early on in the interview that one thing he liked about the comic were the 'little signs' like 'Overacting'. He was referring to a caption in 'Dennis the Menace' where we see Dennis throwing a fit because he thinks Walter's parents have arrived to complain. He shouts, 'Wasn't me! I wasn't near Walter at the time! It couldn't have been me! I . . .' Dennis is leaping in the air, throwing his head back, drops of sweat are flying off his head and his arms are thrown up, his mouth wide open. A little sign, written in red, with an arrow pointing at Dennis says, 'Overacting'.

I asked Isaac, 'Who's saying that?' He didn't know. (My question came before the conversation about the editor.) What is of interest here is that again, unsolicited, (although all I had asked him was what he had liked about *The Beano*) he had selected a highly self-conscious form of writing. Dennis, who at first glance is a character who children are invited to identify with, is here distanced and criticised by another voice. Isaac showed himself to be clearly tickled by this sideways kind of comment. Of course this self-critiquing kind of narrative can be found in many kinds of novels and stories but the pleasure derived in the comic form is that the comment critiques an action from another medium. Dennis is a picture, the comment comes in writing. The use of the different media to make the comment reinforces a separation between the two statements: Dennis in a rage; the truth as revealed by the aside.

Isaac also isolated the pleasure he derived from saying the noises like 'howl' and 'ugh'. I noticed here, that as we read the comic together, he had very fixed ideas about how these noises should be pronounced and corrected me several times especially with 'ugh' and 'heh heh'. He said 'ug' and pronounced the 'eh' of 'heh' as if it were the 'e' of 'egg'. He seemed to like the artificiality of these sounds whereas when I read them out loud I had tried to make them naturalistic; I had tried to make 'ugh' into a naturalistic sound of disgust and 'heh heh' into a kind of giggle. Isaac preferred the idea that these sounds belong to particular kind of 'Beano' talk. In fact, he repeated these sounds as signifiers in his play and conversation away from *The Beano*. If he thinks up some little trick, or he comes up with a good move in chess, he says, 'heh heh'. *The Beano* was giving him a kind of stagey vocabulary, a kind of short-hand to indicate a feeling or an idea. Unlike naturalistic fiction, it has given him a code that stands somewhere between language and gesture that can comment on his own or other people's actions.

Isaac made very few comments about how things were drawn, or why they were drawn in a particular way, but one visual gag which pleased him was where some children burst out of a bathing cap that had been stretched to ludicrous proportions by being put over the end of a chute in a swimming pool. He was not prompted to say anything about the way in which comics switch from close-ups to wide shots and two shots as part of their cinematic language. This was of no interest to him. Nor was he particularly interested in commenting on a page in which photos were mixed with cartoons, where 'The Bash Street Kids' go on a sports day, and we see 'real' children at a sports day being disrupted by the cartoon Bash Street Kids, both *within* the frame of a photo and *between* the frames. Like the 'overacting' sign, this is yet another example of an 'alienation effect' as described by the playwright Bertold Brecht. The comic form intrudes on and breaks up the 'naturalism' of the photos. It draws attention to itself as a constructed device with, say, a frame in

127

which some children are looking inside a sack in a sack race. The child (a photo) is saying, 'Ouch! who put crabs in my sack? Oo! Ow!' A Bash Street Kid appears bottom frame right, head and shoulders, with hand over his mouth saying, (ironically we can assume), 'Hee-hee! I wonder.'

It is, of course, quite absurd for the Bash Street Kids, as comic creations, to have intervened in the lives of these 'real' children but the comic pretends that this is possible. A very pleasing mixture of absurdism, fantasy, wish-fulfilment and mockery is presented here with a nice metalinguistic and metagraphical commentary. I asked Isaac if he would like to be in the photos, hoping that he would enjoy the idea of having the opportunity to be commented on and subverted like that. No, he said, he wouldn't and I thought of those sea-side, life-size comic characters with the hole for holiday-makers to put their faces in. Some people enjoy the absurdity of being the fat bather and the silly policemen and others are embarrassed by the self-demolition involved.

Reader-situational

Isaac's reader-situations are as described on p.124 (on the floor outside the kitchen) but in the interview he made clear some further aspects of his reading behaviour. He said that he read one copy, the new copy, and then 'leaves it for a few weeks'. Then he reads it again. 'If I finish one, I don't read it on the same day [read it again, he means] so I don't get bored with it. I read ones I haven't read recently.' In other words he worked out a system which involved constantly keeping the comics rotating, to keep them fresh. In fact, he had invented his own bibliographic system here, a way of keeping a kind of Beanoland alive. This is particularly important when we bear in mind that all the characters in *The Beano* live in series that imply a reference backwards. When Isaac was very young I had a difficult conversation with him trying to explain that I had read *The Beano* when I was a boy, which meant that if Dennis the Menace was real he would be older than me. At the age of four Isaac was unable to hold the two time-frames in his mind at the same time. Now, at nearly six, he could inhabit that strange permanence of the comic's characters. His bibliographic system informed this permanence and enabled him to flesh out details of their existence, and know more about them. In his own way, he was studying *The Beano*.

Another feature of his reader-situation is that at this time *The Beano* had virtually supplanted all other forms of fiction. Up to the age of five, Isaac wanted to be read to every night, and chose books from piles of picture books and folk stories that came into the house for me to review. When he became a 'Beano' student, he very clearly said that he did not want to be read to any more and he stopped going to the picture book shelves when he was looking for something to read. *The Beano* became all. I have not witnessed this with any of my other children and have, as yet, no satisfactory explanation for it. It was sudden, determined and still held some six months later. However, the situation was complicated by an obsession with non-fiction material usually to do with wildlife and dinosaurs. Some of his bibliographic skills and cross-referencing were transferred to non-fiction books and he compared pictures of elephants from one encyclopedia with another, just as he cross-referred in conversation between one episode of a 'Beano' character and another.

Structural

In the interview we read one copy of *The Beano* together (May 22 1993) and I interposed some structural questions. I put it to him that most of the stories seemed to be about people who were naughty. This was a generalisation he would not buy, and he pointed out that Les Pretend just makes things up and rotten things happen to Calamity James. However, this leaves the rest of the comic: Dennis the Menace and Gnasher, Billy Whizz, Gnasher and Gnipper, Minnie the Minx, Danny's Nanny. The Yeti with Betty, Number 13, The Bash Street Kids, Smudge, Ball Boy, The Germs, Ivy the Terrible, and Roger the Dodger which have naughtiness or, at least errors that involve grown-ups interpreting errors as naughtiness, as their central theme. It is worth noting here that *The Beano* most definitely avoids closure and recuperation. In this issue's episode of Dennis the Menace and Gnasher, Dennis' ruse is to get Walter to recite some of his own poetry. This is so 'soppy' that it puts Dennis' parents to sleep. This means Dennis can now offer Walter a game of 'chess played in the kitchen' which turns out to be Dennis charging at Walter with a broomstick on the checked kitchen floor-covering. 'This is "Menace Style" chess! Charge!' shouts Dennis, and this is the last frame of the strip. No slipper-wielding parents move in to give Dennis his come-uppance.

There is, then, an element in *The Beano* that a child of Isaac's age will be hard pushed to find replicated in 'children's literature', where the respectability of the form seems to entail naughtiness being contained within punishment or unwanted and unhappy consequences. It is difficult to say how important this is, but one can surmise that the wish-fulfilment aspect here is very strong.

Ideological

This area of discussion comes within the orbit of ideology and in the interview I raised this matter with reference to Calamity James. He, as I have said, is someone to whom calamities happen. This particular episode involves him falling for a 'gorgeous' blonde. This means that he takes up weight training which wins him the girl, who is delighted – 'Wahoo! I've found a boyfriend at last!' The choric figure of Alexander Lemming interjects, 'She likes James? But . . .?' and in the final frame, the blonde bursts out of her heavy duty armoured corsets and her industrial strength support tights. The consequence is that a great wobbly belly appears ('Wobble! Blubber!') and big fat legs. James rushes off – 'Help! Save me!' and Alexander comments, 'Just his luck!'

Clearly, various stereotypes are brought to play here, the main one being the rapacious but ugly woman that no man in his right mind would fancy. Isaac, not surprisingly, was mystified by this story. He usually liked the strip, 'he's always unlucky' but this one 'wasn't that funny'. I tried to find out what he understood about it. I asked him what he thought the corset was for and he said, 'to make it look as if she's got big tits'. I deduced from this that he was able to read the beauty-into-beast transformation that the woman goes through and so perhaps he understood more than he was letting on. I asked him what he thought the moral was, but the word was not in his consciousness and even though I tried to explain what I meant he was not forthcoming. The story is objectionable from an adult point of view for several reasons: in general terms the humour derives from deriding victims, where the usual source of humour in *The Beano* is from the come-uppance or the downfall of privilege, power, snobbery and spoilsports. However, the girl in this episode is simply ugly and so falls into a situation that Isaac described as 'unlucky'.

By and large *The Beano* avoids sexual relations; girls appear as naughty equivalents to boys, (see Minnie the Minx), but in Number 13, Frankie (Frankenstein's monster) has been invited to a ball. He hasn't got a girlfriend to take so Frankenstein makes him one. At the ball, they dance so fiercely that she falls apart – 'Mabel went to pieces – must have been my good looks that did it,' says Frankie. Frankenstein is annoyed. This seems to fit the normal 'Beano' requirement of an episode that goes wrong with a parent figure being annoyed or downgraded in some way. One can possibly read unconscious sexual undertones in dancing so vigorously that the female creature falls apart, which of course slots into the stereotype of the voracious male who is so active that he destroys women. This piece of male self-flattery is partly demolished by the apparent folly of Frankie's pun 'Mabel went to pieces' and the fact that he attributes this to his 'good looks' whereas we all *know* that he is ugly.

Reader-responsive

Isaac was quite clear about his preferences. The best was The Germs and second-best Roger the Dodger. I am fairly sure that when he first started reading *The Beano* he would have said his favourite character was Dennis the Menace. He loved the rhyme in the name, he used the word 'menacing' to indicate being naughty and he was once fond of his Dennis the Menace badge. However, the rise in ratings for these other two strips seems to represent a careful selection. The Germs is a particularly inventive strip where Iris the Virus, Jeremy Germ and Ugly Jack Bacteria invade various parts of Ill Will's body. The interest here is the invention with which the cartoonist can provide the 'real' explanation of sore throats, sore joints and the rest within the fantasy of talking-germs. I would guess that there is something quite satisfying to a small child to see his or her illnesses 'explained' in such personified and funny ways. It is a kind of mock demystification told in terms of naughtiness. In this particular episode, the germs make poor Ill Will's back ache, so he gulps down some castor oil. The germs then bobsleigh on the oil down to Ill Will's 'tum'. 'Ooh . . .' says Will, 'I think I've had too much castor oil . . .' Next frame: 'Waaaa!' Sign reads: 'Will's bathroom,' with an arrow pointing and the germs in the 'reveal-box' that the artist draws for them, say, 'Chortle! We've given Will Runny Tummy!'

The story provides a totally logical but absurd explanation for diarrhoea, though I was a little disappointed, I confess, that Isaac thought a runny tummy simply signified 'throwing up'. However, his satisfaction, it struck me, comes from these naughty germs doing the business inside Will's – and by implication – his own tummy. I noticed that on various occasions in the previous year he asked us about germs and in its own way, the strip created a picture that is in one sense unbelievable, but in another way not totally divorced from the scientific narrative of bacteria fighting battles with white blood corpuscles.

Narrative-competence/repertoire/intertextuality

I have already addressed the question of narrative competence in the way in which, for example, Isaac enjoys the editorial asides like 'overacting'. However, in going through the comic, story by story, he let out various comments which implied and suggested the kind of reading experience he brought to *The Beano* both from past issues and other sources. He could read the difference between the different voices in the comic such as 'thinks', narrative continuation words: 'later' etc., sound effects that float mid-air around events, characters' speeches, titles, signs and so on. It was clear from talking with him that any individual issue of *The Beano* exists in relation to all other Beanos and Beano annuals, so that when talking about Minnie the Minx he broke off to recount a whole episode of the character in a previous comic. This bit of story telling lasted several minutes and was done in order to prove that Minnie the Minx is 'sort of naughty'. When we talked about Les Pretend, I had some difficulty following what actually happened. In the final frame, a man throws a broken boat up into a tree. I was rather sceptical about this, so Isaac said, 'It's only a comic, it's not true.' So I said, 'How do you know?' He replied, 'Cos dogs can't talk.'

This level of handling metalanguage has partly come from reading *The Beano*, but also from a great deal of role play, other reading, play-going, Pollock's Paper Theatre-watching at home and so on. He brought a sense of the artificiality of all fictional forms to *The Beano* and was happy to collaborate with its creators in enjoying the strips.

As well as reading the various codes and understanding that they are
different voices, he could also read the typographical hints which guide a
reader on mood, tempo and pitch. As I was reading out part of Dennis
the Menace, he corrected me by saying, 'Whenever you see big letters it's
loud.' I am not sure where he picked up this piece of competence, perhaps
from older brothers and sisters, but whatever its source, he has acquired
an increasingly important aspect of public writing: that its shape, colour
and size all help to construct its audience.

When we talked about Number 13, he was very keen to tell me the names
of all the characters. The significance of this was that in this particular
episode, only one name was mentioned – Frankie. 'In fact,' said Isaac,
'there's Boris, Dad, Wolfie, Mum, Tiddles and Ghost.' This kind of
expertise has come from his 'study' sessions when praying outside the
kitchen door. It means that each episode is encased in a context of
reference and expectation, as when he says (see above) 'Calamity James is
always unlucky', or 'Smiffy's got a really hard head' and 'Winston is the
Janitor's cat.'

The process of initiation was particularly visible on the page for the
Dennis the Menace fan club. Here were some classic jokes, some of which
he understood, others which he did not. The 'star prize' this week went
to: 'I feel like a tea bag, I've been in and out of hot water all day! Har-har!'
Isaac did not understand this one, not knowing or not remembering the
phrase 'in hot water'. However, he criticised the joke of a caveman who
said, 'No, you can't ring Sharon – the phone hasn't been invented yet!'
This was 'just a copy of a previous joke,' Isaac said, 'where someone said
the car hadn't been invented yet.' Again, it is intertextuality and an
awareness of structure and meaning that caused this joke to fail, but then
The Beano team probably do not assume that any individual reader of *The
Beano* has a bank of previous issues to draw on.

As we have already seen, Isaac cross-references within *The Beano* in terms
of whether people are as naughty as each other and this also applies to
'softness'. Walter, he observes is a 'softy' like Cuthbert in The Bash Street
Kids. A 'softy', according to Isaac is someone who is 'always right, not
naughty'. The multi-narrative form of a comic enables him to generalise
about stereotypes, comparing and contrasting different characters and

133

storylines. There is a sense here, as with the asides and the switching and contrasting of codes, in which *The Beano* draws its readers' attentions to narrative itself. The comic has enabled Isaac to generalise and theorise about crucial aspects of narratology.

I was also interested to find out if any of these ideas have a shared currency with school friends, and whether there is a kind of intertextual reservoir that is drawn on in games, conversation, jokes and the like. Charlie and Sophie, two children in school, also pledged to be keen followers of *The Beano*. It seemed they talked about different stories together. I should say here, that according to Isaac, he was the initiator: 'I asked Charlie if he had *The Beano* and he said, "No", so I said, just get one to see how you like it.' This is a fine example of how 'reading' is also about 'knowing how to read.' His advice to Charlie is not simply the encouraging comment about how such-and-such a book or comic is worth reading. His comment is strategic, as if to say, this is the kind of thing you need to do if you want to find out if something is worth reading. This kind of comment speaks volumes about how children learn to read, which is so much more than learning to say letters and words. It is interesting that Isaac was able to produce such a strategic comment about *The Beano*, almost as if he were accepting or conceding that it is a genre unlike school books and one that has to be learnt. As an experienced reader of *The Beano*, he was offering up some of his expertise. As far as I could make out, this was taken in good part by Charlie, and jokes and stories were thenceforth shared over sandwiches and drinks at lunchtime.

Conclusion

Reading *The Beano* is a complex process, operating at various levels both within its text and backwards to previous issues. It calls on various kinds of sophistication in picking up messages, codes, structures and meanings that are not immediately apparent. Some six months or so later, (at the time of writing this chapter) Isaac had become less obsessed about *The Beano* but it is quite clear how his activity and thought has fed into his reading.

The cross-referencing systems that he taught himself are now fed into non-fiction reading about animals and plants. He compares what different books and texts say about the same creature. With fiction, it has given him a confidence that I have not observed with any of my other children. Basically, he thinks that any text is readable. It can be small print or large, illustrated or not, one page, several pages or a novel. As far as he is concerned, if it is in print, he is entitled to read it. Six months after this interview, he was slowly and painstakingly reading *The Lion, the Witch and the Wardrobe.*

It is very easy to underestimate the complexity of what readers of comics have to do to understand and enjoy them. In the event of these being very young readers, comics can provide a wide platform of knowledge and skill, most, perhaps all, of which is usable in other literary and graphic forms. The comics provided Isaac with a massive back-referencing reservoir as well as an autonomy. These two kinds of awareness strike me as vital for turning children into readers. What is significant is that in the right kind of circumstances, children can teach themselves how to do this.

10

'Madam! Read the scary book, Madam': Momahl and her picture books – the emergent bilingual reader

Helen Bromley

For the second time, Helen Bromley opens her classroom door and shows the reader that bilingual learners are as capable of reading pictures as mother-tongue speakers. She goes on to trace one young bilingual learner's apprenticeship with reading and the crucial role played by picture books in her development. Helen Bromley also stresses the important networking that goes on as early as the reception year, where young readers share their passion for picture books with one another. In this chapter we see how picture books teach many reading lessons effortlessly: in the words of Margaret Meek we observe how texts teach what readers learn. We also enjoy Momahl's exuberant and demanding personality, as she makes her early steps towards independent reading in a second language, demonstrating for us some of the skills and secrets learned by accomplished young readers of pictorial texts.

Momahl did not call me, Miss; she did not call me teacher, or even Mrs Bromley; She called me Madam. In doing so, she not only gave me a new label, she also demonstrated quite forcefully that she was a rule breaker. She arrived in my reception classroom in January, four months after the arrival of the rest of the children. Consequently she entered a classroom world where, although many freedoms existed for the children, many rules and customs had become a well established part of the daily routine. One such routine was storytime, the way the classroom day began. In the short time that Momahl was with us before she returned to Pakistan, she was to re-shape storytime for all those involved.

Each morning as the children came into school with their parents, they would listen to a story, take leave of their carers and sit on the carpet to read a book, either on their own or with a friend. Although she never arrived with an adult from her own family, Momahl would always be included in one of the reading groups and could often be seen queuing up by the side of one of the mothers, trying to push her selected book to the fore. She quickly initiated herself into one of the 'literacy events' of the school and, in doing so, rapidly became part of the community of readers in our classroom. As far as the other children were concerned, she was a member of their own particular branch of the 'literacy club'.

Books which featured paper engineering were amongst Momahl's favourites. It was in observing her with these books that I first noticed the way in which her peers supported her in the cultural practices surrounding picture books. For example, Jodie showed Momahl how to lift the flaps in one book, shouting 'Boo!' as she did so. Although there were times in the following weeks when I was to regret this particular example of scaffolded learning, (cries of Boo! resounding around the room) I was nevertheless pleased at both the teaching and learning that had taken place between these two children. Jodie had instinctively chosen one of the linguistic strategies likely to be familiar across all cultures, the turn-taking game of peek a boo, and applied it to the shared context of the picture book. As time wore on, Jodie seemed to have decided that Momahl was ready to take on more extended reading and taught her the title phrase 'Look out! He's behind you'. In this instance, Jodie was the expert, kindly and intelligently leading Momahl's reading of the written text. Soon, a situation was to occur where the roles were to be reversed.

The practice of sharing picture books on an individual basis with the children was already well established. It was during one of these sessions that I began to realise how good Momahl was at reading pictures. I had the opportunity to share *Each Peach Pear Plum*[1] with Momahl and Katy, another girl who had recently arrived in my class. I read the book to them, encouraging them to find the characters in the pictures, as I had done many times before. It soon became clear, from Momahl's reaction to the book, that she was able to understand many of the Ahlbergs' literary jokes. Her favourite page was that of 'Bo Peep up the hill, I spy Jack and

Jill.' When she saw this page, Momahl immediately sang the nursery rhyme, Jack and Jill, in its entirety. This was before she had heard the page read to her. This meant that she was able to identify the essential clues to their identity from the picture. She also used the opportunity to sing other rhymes to us, some in English and some in Urdu. The picture book clearly provided a context in which Momahl could demonstrate prior knowledge of text. Katy was not yet able to make such links. However, she was determined to say the rhymes and began to learn Jack and Jill and Little Bo Peep with Momahl's help.

Each Peach Pear Plum was to become Momahl's first known text. The reasons for this seemed to be closely connected with the nature of the book itself. It is a text that places heavy reliance on rhyme and rhythm. These two factors supported Momahl's reading, providing her with a strong tune on the page to follow. Momahl also spent a long time looking at the pictures, spotting the characters, singing the rhymes that she knew and guessing those that she did not. An example of this was her reaction to the page that showed Baby Bunting. For this page she sang Rock a Bye Baby, the most appropriate rhyme that she knew. (I have had experience of children with English as a first language making a similar substitution.) It is important to note that Momahl was by no means fluent in English, though she could recite the alphabet, count to twenty and label many objects. It was in the art of discourse that she was not so skilled. However, picture books were to help her go some way towards overcoming this problem and give her powers of negotiation where she had previously had none.

One of Momahl's particular skills was reading emotion from the illustrations in picture books. It is unlikely that any of the books in the classroom were familiar to her, yet she happily used illustrations to categorise the texts. The particular book which first drew my attention to this ability was a traditional tale called *The Hobyahs*.[2] This book was popular with the children in my class because of its structure, the parts that they could join in with and their fascination with the hobyahs themselves, drawn in such a way to make the children curious about them. This particular day was the first time that Momahl had seen the book and when she saw the illustrations she called out 'Scary book, scary book.' This interpretation was very apt. The plot involves the hobyahs kidnapping a child and carrying her off in a hobyah bag (see figure 23). The pictures are abstract which made Momahl's understanding all the more remarkable. She was not reading pictures of frightened people, which in itself would have been clever, but pictures of imaginary monsters. None of the children already in my class would have made such a judgement so explicit. They were aware of the cultural norms of the classroom; Momahl was not. Although questioning and comments were encouraged, the children were used to going through a particular ritual each time that a story was read. We would read the title, the publisher and any dedication made by the author before the story began. Momahl was not aware of the need to observe such rules and consequently broke them.

I was so impressed with Momahl's reaction to the book, that I praised her profusely, whilst the rest of the class sat on the carpet rather bemused by my obvious excitement. Jodie decided to try to find out what was going on, 'What has she done Mrs. Bromley?' she asked. I told the class that Momahl was very clever because she had read the pictures. One boy, Christopher, said, 'You don't read pictures, you read words.' An exciting

"HOBYAH! HOBYAH! HOBYAH!
Tear down the turnip house!
Chase off the old man!
Chase off the old woman!
Put the little girl in the Hobyah bag!"

Then Little Dog Turpie
wriggled and thumped
and bounced and bumped,
but try as he might
he could not get out of the turnip box.

Figure 23 From *The Hobyahs* by Simon Stern, published by Methuen

and intelligent discussion then followed, with many of the children making explicit their knowledge about how pictures supported them in their reading and how information about the story could be gained from looking at them. Hannah made the contribution that 'sometimes the pictures tell a different story to the words.' Asked to give an example of this, she replied, 'You know, like in *Lily Takes a Walk*.'[3] This was a very good example indeed. We had read this book several times as a class but had not made this aspect of its structure explicit. Had Momahl been aware that it was not the norm to call out and label the books, just as the story was beginning, then this opportunity for the children to distance themselves from their own knowledge would not have occurred.

All of the interactions between Momahl, the children and the picture books seem to me to be examples of scaffolded learning. The features of successful scaffolding within a *formal setting* have been outlined by Wood, Bruner and Ross.[4] They are:

- reducing the size of the task to something manageable for the child;
- keeping the child 'in the field' and motivated;
- marking critical or relevant features;
- 'modelling' the task.

Although the interactions outlined above were not taking place in a formal setting, such features were clearly identifiable. The picture book provides an ideal opportunity for such learning to take place as joint reading of a text gives all involved an opportunity to share their particular expertise. The children were all working within a 'zone of proximal development', with more capable readers attempting more challenging reading.

Jodie was particularly adept at marking critical and relevant features such as the flaps in *Look Out He's Behind You*.[5] In showing Momahl how to use the flaps, Jodie clearly marked them for her and demonstrated to Momahl how an experienced reader would approach such a task.

As a teacher it was interesting to watch the way in which Momahl herself scaffolded learning for other children in my class. Again, picture books formed the context in which the learning took place. Momahl showed Katy her knowledge of intertextual links and the pleasure that comes from sharing secrets with the author, two very important lessons to learn about reading. Momahl's obvious delight in the repeated reading of the classic Ahlberg text *Each Peach Pear Plum* kept Katy motivated to try out such readings for herself. Momahl placed such importance on the illustrations, because the written text was not accessible to her, but her response to the pictures opened up new ways of reading for the rest of the class.

Momahl had also developed her own strategy for participating in the shared context that was story time. Shirley Brice Heath states that children from minority cultures need to learn or employ a variety of strategies for reading in order to be successful in early literacy. In the article, 'What no bedtime story means', she lists the ways in which one group of minority children 'will have to learn to extend its labelling habits to other domains, learn distinctions in discourse strategies and structures and become active information givers within a participant frame of reference to books.'[6] This describes Momahl's behaviour perfectly. Having been praised for labelling the scary book, she continued to offer a label for most of the books that were read to the class during the weeks that she was with us. Each label was entirely appropriate. For example, *Not Now Bernard*[7] joined *The Hobyahs* in the scary book category, whilst *Gorilla*[8] was a monkey book and *All Join In*[9] a singing book. The category that appealed to her the most was that of friendly books. This label was first offered to *Kipper's Toybox*[10] by Mick Inkpen and subsequently to every Mick Inkpen book that was read to the class. It is perhaps easy to see how she might transfer this label to other books about Kipper the dog, but what I found more interesting was that it was transferred to all the books about Jasper the cat[11] and to other Mick Inkpen books such as *One Bear at Bedtime*[12] and *LullabyHullabaloo.*[13] No book by any other author/illustrator entered the friendly book category. This shows that Momahl was able to recognise the characteristics of Mick Inkpen's drawings, remember them and transfer that knowledge to new contexts.

Eve Gregory[14] describes how negotiation was a critical factor in becoming a reader for Tajul, a boy for whom English was a second language. She describes negotiation in three ways:

- to confer, consult together, take advice;
- to compromise or meet half way;
- to overcome a difficulty.

I have attempted to apply the same categories to Momahl's reading behaviour. One of the first negotiations that Momahl had to make was that of joining in shared reading, first thing each morning. Her behaviour demonstrated that she knew the ingredients required for successful shared reading – an adult and a picture book! In placing herself next to an adult reading with a child, she clearly demonstrated her willingness to participate in such an activity and was rapidly absorbed into it. Momahl was equally successful in negotiating a role in other forms of shared reading, in small groups or as an individual with the teacher. In her reading of *Each Peach Pear Plum* she read the pictures in a way that made her knowledge of traditional rhymes both in Urdu and English readily accessible to the teacher. In choosing to read the pictures she successfully negotiated an appropriate reading of the text for herself.

Writing about shared reading, Eve Gregory states that 'there are certain rules . . . boundaries which delineate the event.' The same is true for story time. In calling out and labelling the books at the beginning of such sessions, Momahl knowingly crossed such boundaries. Nobody seeing her mischievous face could deny that she was also participating in the special type of rule-bound play that is story reading. As Gregory says 'Sometimes playfulness and wondering and the resulting language of hypothesis are fully acceptable.' They certainly were in this case.

Like Tajul in Gregory's study, Momahl generated hypotheses, particularly about pictures. The cultural practice that was central to Momahl's success as a reader was the sharing of high quality picture books. From the incidents outlined above it is obvious that the pictures were crucial to Momahl's success in, and definition of, what being a reader entailed. With the support of her classmates as well as her class teacher, boundaries for the reading of stories were re-negotiated in an atmosphere where she could not fail. A new way of talking about picture books emerged. We were to get used to her demands for us to 'Read the scary book, Madam.'

On one particular occasion, Momahl was visited in class by the advisory teacher for bilingual children. She had come to assess Momahl's language skills. As part of her assessment she wanted to read with Momahl and offered a choice of several books. One was a bilingual text, two or three obviously referred to Momahl's background, and one was *Kipper* by Mick

Inkpen.[15] I watched from a distance to see which book Momahl would choose. There was no hesitation; she chose *Kipper*. In discussion afterwards, the advisory teacher expressed her disappointment that Momahl had so blatantly rejected her own culture. On the other hand, I thought that it was rather clever of Momahl, faced with sharing a book with a stranger to choose, out of all her categories, a *friendly* book.

On the day that Momahl left us to return to Pakistan, she would not leave without her book-bag, however hard we tried to dissuade her. She took with her *Look Out He's Behind You*, *Jasper's Beanstalk* and *The Hobyahs*. I would like to think that this was no coincidence. These books and others like them have shown me the importance of picture books for bilingual children. In labelling and reading the books so effectively, Momahl not only succeeded as a reader herself, but opened up new horizons for the children in my class. The books were returned to us, several days later, by one of Momahl's relations with a message thanking us for all that we had done. I felt it was the other way round and that Momahl deserved thanks for her playful demands to 'Read the scary book, Madam', teaching us that when reading the pictures, language is universal.

References

1 Janet and Allan Ahlberg, *Each Peach Pear Plum*. London: Kestrel, 1978.

2 Simon Stern, *The Hobyahs*. London: Methuen, 1977.

3 Satoshi Kitamura, *Lily Takes a Walk*. London: Blackie, 1987.

4 Wood, Bruner and Ross (1976) in Eve Gregory, 'Negotiation as a Critical Factor in Learning to Read in a Second Language' in Graddol, Maybin and Stierer, (eds) *Researching Language and Literacy in a Social Context*. Milton Keynes: Multilingual Matters Ltd in association with The Open University, 1994.

5 Tony Bradman and Margaret Chamberlain, *Look Out, He's Behind You*! London: Little Mammoth, 1989.

6 Shirley Brice Heath in Eve Gregory, 1994, op. cit.

7 David McKee, *Not Now Bernard*. London: Anderson Press, 1980.

8 Anthony Browne, *Gorilla*. London: Julia MacRae, 1983.

9 Quentin Blake, *All Join In*. London: Jonathan Cape, 1990.

10 Mick Inkpen, *Kipper's Toybox*. London: Hodder Children's Books, 1992.

11 Nick Butterworth and Mick Inkpen, *Jasper's Beanstalk*. London: Picture Knight, 1993.

12 Mick Inkpen, *One Bear at Bedtime*. London: Hodder Children's Books, 1987.

13 Mick Inkpen, *LullabyHullabaloo*. London: Hodder and Stoughton, 1993.

14 Eve Gregory, op. cit.

15 Mick Inkpen, *Kipper*. London: Hodder and Stoughton, 1991.

11

The left-handed reader – linear sentences and unmapped pictures

Victor Watson

The title says it all: in this chapter Victor Watson probes ever more deeply into one six-year-old's unusual journey into reading. (We have already met her in Chapters 6 and 8.) Ann was a gifted reader of pictorial texts from an early age, but was slow to turn her attention to the printed word. We watch Ann's tentative steps towards becoming a reader; we are charmed by her intuitive understanding of complicated ideas conveyed through pictures, when she was only four; we note her need to re-read familiar texts over and over again a year later; we worry that the words lag behind the pictures in her reading at age six (though we should know better – for some children it takes longer for no apparent reason); we waver for a moment in our conviction that these texts (and good teaching) will enable Ann to master print; we wonder if her fascination for pictures is getting in the way; we sigh with relief when she reads the printed text successfully, but share Victor Watson's hunch that something has been (inevitably) lost. His final chapter shows what a teacher, with time to work individually with children, time to reflect and time to listen, can achieve. Victor Watson has extended our understanding of young children learning to read as well as illustrating the liberating and fruitful outcomes when children engage with outstanding texts within a supportive environment.

Most new readers confidently address pictures with an inventive and free-wheeling readiness to speculate. They seem untroubled by mysteries and uncertainties. Many adults, on the other hand, are inclined to feel more comfortable if there is a title, or a caption, which helps them to get a conceptual grasp of the picture. Most of us need words; words have a primary authority. Think of your own habits when you see a

145

Victorian genre painting, or any kind of narrative illustration. Do you not instantly read the caption or title? You could manage without it, of course, but the words provide you with a way of reading the picture. But beginning readers have no such inhibitions and do not need the explanations that words make possible. For example, although I have always admired *Outside Over There* [1], it puzzles and irritates me that Sendak has included in one of the closing illustrations the figure of Mozart playing a keyboard instrument in a summerhouse. This seems bizarre, and I would like an explanation [2] because I am an adult reader who dislikes loose ends. Ann, on the other hand, when I pointed at Mozart and asked who he was, replied calmly that it was Ida's grandad.

This is the story of Ann. It is also the story of the questions and misgivings that she provoked in me. When I first met her, Ann was only four years old and very conscious that she was the youngest and smallest child in the school. Her low voice was often little more than a whisper, except when she was with her friend Sadie (see also Chapters 6 and 8). She was a grave little person with an appealing diminutive dignity and self-possession. She would gaze at a single picture for ages, and was happy to discuss its details with me far beyond the patience of any of her peers. She was often tired and very easily distracted, except when we were talking about pictures. She always chose her favourite books from my box – mostly those by Anthony Browne. When she was excited about a particular illustration, she stammered breathlessly in her eagerness to tell me what she was thinking.

She loved pictures but showed no interest in words. At first, this did not trouble me, but when the months and terms went by and she *still* showed no dutiful interest in the words on the page, I began to ask myself whether her extraordinary ability to read pictures in some way 'worked against' her reading words. The contrast between her remarkable ability to read the one, and her inability – or reluctance – to read the other, was baffling. We talk of 'reading' words and 'reading' pictures as if they are similar activities. But are they? Jane Doonan [3] thinks not and prefers to use the term 'beholder' for anyone 'with formal understanding of visual images that are . . . sequences of scenes, comic-book frames, illustrations in books.' She explains, 'To call such a person a reader, and the skill visual literacy, would be convenient but fails to acknowledge the difference between the ways we receive written words and pictorial images.' I am sure she is right to insist upon the distinction – but it is little help to me because Ann certainly had no 'formal understanding' of visual images. She was both a 'beginning reader' and a 'beginning beholder'.

The syntax of sentences provides order, sequence and coherence. To put it at its most basic, a new reader can decipher a sentence in only one direction. But what kinds of syntax do pictures have? Can their details be read in any order, or entirely disregarded? Does this selective or unstructured 'reading' depend on merely arbitrary eye-movements, or do young readers develop private reading 'systems' for dealing with detailed imagery and the dimensional spaciousness of pictures?

When we share picture books with new readers, they may seem to be capable of indicating only what they have noticed, of playing the age-old naming game. They point at details, or simply label them, saying 'Look! There's a duck.' But, although this activity seems to involve only a process for making pictorial inventories, I learned from working with a number of children over several years – and from Ann in particular – that labelling quickly develops into interpretation; and furthermore that this qualitative process of image analysis opens up ways towards implicit recognition of irony, humour, perspective, and flashback. I believe, too, that the nature of the interpretation – the quality of the reading – depends to a great extent on the imagery and style of the picture book.

On my fourth visit to the school, Ann chose Anthony Browne's *The Tunnel*[4] from my box. She could not read any words, and so I read the text and she talked to me about the pictures. I was taping our conversation. The story concerns a brother and sister who dislike each other's company, until the boy gets trapped in a fantasy world and is paralysed in stone. The sister overcomes her fear and goes to rescue him. Anthony Browne is uncompromising here: the girl rescues her brother by putting her arms around him and hugging him. This story is about courage and love. Ann noticed that on the final endpaper the boy's football and his sister's story-book are side by side. I showed her the opening endpaper, where I had observed that there is the story-book, but no football. I asked her why the author had done the two endpapers differently.

147

■ **Ann**   There's the girl's book and the boy's . . . football.
  VW   But at the front of the book there's no football. Only the little
          girl's book. Why do you think that is? Why do you think the man
          who made the book put them side by side at the end like that?
  Ann   Because . . . at the end they were kind . . . and at the beginning
          they weren't.   ■

I thought that was remarkable. The story says nothing explicit about love
and reconciliation; it works entirely through suggestion. But that small
detail – the placing of the boy's ball close to his sister's book – is a precise
pictorial metaphor expressing the story's theme of reconciliation, and Ann
(though she called it being 'kind') recognised this. Her observation
became explicitly interpretative and took her, through symbol and
metaphor, to an understanding of theme.[5] If there had been a final
illustration showing the brother and sister holding hands, Ann's
observation would have been a precise response to a merely literal
representation. But to understand that the football and the book 'stood
for' their owners and, in addition, that their proximity 'stood for'
reconciliation, was a genuinely interpretative insight involving a double
reading of metaphor.

This particular interpretation involved more than an instant revelation
about an image; it involved a kind of 'backward reading' and the ability to
hold in her mind a full and holistic sense of the story and the way the
narrative web is strung together. I had asked Ann why the brother looked
unhappy in one of the earlier pictures. At first she hesitated and said, 'I
can't guess.' But then she said, 'I know, because . . . he didn't want her to
come with him.'

This perception probably informed her experience of the rest of the story.
What cannot be known is the extent to which her understanding was
prompted by my invitation. This was probably not a case of an implicit
understanding being made into an explicit comment, for her admission ('I
can't guess') seems to indicate that she had not thought about it at all. As
always with Ann, this perception seemed to leap fully-formed into her
understanding, instantly modifying everything else.

When she turned to a new picture, Ann began a complex mental process

– a kind of narrative mapping. We can see it happening in the following transcript of a conversation we had that same afternoon about Anthony Browne's big double-page illustration of the forest (see figure 24).

Figure 24 **From *The Tunnel* by Anthony Browne, published by Julia MacRae Books**

Ann There's a secret door there.
VW It does seem like a secret door. Where do you think it leads to?
Ann . . . A witch's house.
VW Is that a witch's house.
Ann I think so.
VW Why do you think so?
Ann Because it's all dark in that window.
VW Oh, so it is, yes. What do you think of this tree?
Ann . . . . That's a pig.
VW It does look like a pig, doesn't it, yes.
Ann Yes.
VW What about this tree? . . . What about this one? Have you noticed anything strange about that tree?
Ann No?
VW You haven't?

Ann	Yes, that's a wolf holding a walking-stick.
VW	Is it a wolf holding a walking-stick or is it a tree?
Ann	It's a wolf.
VW	Is it?
Ann	Yes, look. That's the eyes and that's the walking-stick.
VW	Do you think she knows there's a wolf nearby?
Ann	No.
VW	What do you think she's feeling? Is she feeling happy?
Ann	No.
VW	How can you tell?
Ann	Because . . . she's got a sad face.
VW	She has, hasn't she? Why is that red all like that?
Ann	Because she's rushing, fast.
VW	Why do you think she's rushing?
Ann	Because she's frightened of that . . . that bear.
VW	I wouldn't be at all surprised . . . oh, the bear! You didn't mention the bear. There's a bear there! Yes.
Ann	I . . . saw the bear.

Ann, at age four, had the young child's eye for detail. The 'secret door' is probably in fact a tombstone, but her reading of it enabled her to make a narrative link with the house which is behind and above it in the illustration. Some complex narrative mapping was going on here, as Ann strung together the idea of mystery, dark windows, a secret door[6], and probably a memory of *Hansel and Gretel*, and inferred quite appropriately that a witch lived in the cottage. She observed the boar ('That's a pig'), but did not seem to notice anything about the other tree until I asked her about it. Then she spotted the wolf with the walking-stick. This perception was not of the same order as, say, her identifying a picture of a horse in an alphabet book; Anthony Browne's wolf is uncompromisingly a *fairytale* wolf[7] – and Ann's recognition of it came to her because of other pictures she must have seen. She thought she read sadness in the heroine's face, and she already knew one of the pictorial conventions for indicating movement. Making explicit the fact that Rose was 'rushing fast' led her to go back and modify her earlier comment about sadness: she was now clear that Rose was 'frightened' – and that peception, in turn, led back to the other tree on the left-hand page, in which she had presumably already seen the bear without saying so. Carefully, unhurriedly and creatively, Ann's thinking – prompted by my questions – moved over the page, and back and forth within the book, and in and out of her own life, to select and identify constellations of meaning. Reading illustrations was not a mere list-making activity, or an inventorying of her observations; it was a complex and dynamic process, mediated through conversation, as Ann coolly spun her narrative web.

It has become a commonplace to suggest that children quickly become able to observe more details than adult readers. Jan Ormerod reports that adults fail to notice the adventurous baby in *Chicken Licken*[8] until it has climbed onto the stage, but pre-readers see it at once.[9] In my experience this is true, and most contemporary illustrators provide for this facility. The picture on the page becomes a framed treasure-chest of details to be discovered and recognised, to be delved into in no pre-ordained sequence and with no predictable outcome. But Ann showed repeatedly that this delving was also a shaping, and that she brought to the activity her own private reading processes of interpretative thought.

The syntax of sentences and of narrative does not come as a surprise to new readers; they have been speaking syntactically for a good deal of their lives. But it is worth reminding ourselves that the syntax of pictures will not be familiar to all children. One reader newly arrived in a reception class, when showing me a page of *The Snowman*[10], shouted in great excitement, 'There's a snowman! And there's another one! And another!' – and so on, pointing eagerly at each illustration. He had yet to learn that the syntax of this particular kind of picture book requires a reader to know that there are many pictures but only one snowman. The same young reader had another syntactical difficulty – he did not yet understand about directionality and pictures in frames: he thought that the two frames showing Brighton pier were one picture of 'a broken bridge'.

New readers must learn some pictorial semantics too; I once shared *Rosie's Walk*[11] with a four-year-old boy in a reception class, who told me the fox was going to hurt himself on the 'prickles' (see figure 25). This young reader had not yet learnt that 'prickles' in this case were a pictorial convention indicating ripples on the surface of water, and so he was unable to 'see' a pond in his reading of the story. I was not too distressed by this: because of his grasp of the narrative context, he was still able to

Figure 25 From *Rosie's Walk* by Pat Hutchins, published by Bodley Head

predict that the fox was about to experience an uncomfortable catastrophe – but a sharp one instead of a wet one.

Ann, however, had no such difficulties. A week later, she again chose *The Tunnel* but this time her friend Sadie was with her (see Chapter 8). This proved to be very interesting. It was the first time Sadie had seen the book, and so Ann was able to take on the role of an interpreter for her friend. Sadie made a number of observations about the pictures and the almost inaudible Ann instantly became a didactic teacher as if to the manner born. Sadie commented that she didn't think Rose wanted to go into the tunnel – and Ann immediately explained. 'She doesn't want to go in there because she hates the dark, and it's dark in there!' Ann here was relating detail to theme: this is a story partly about overcoming fear. She remembered that earlier in the story we had been told that Rose's brother sometimes 'crept into her room to frighten her, for he knew that she was afraid of the dark.' Ann made other 'linking' observations too: she had noticed that Rose leaves her story book outside the tunnel and *open at a page with a picture of a witch*. She speculated that the witch might have got out of the book, and there was probably in her mind an unspoken thought that it was this witch who lived in the forest cottage in the later picture.

There was something going on here which was a great deal more than mere labelling, or list-making. I repeatedly have the feeling that my tapes reveal only a fraction of this young reader's complex ability to structure narrative from pictures. For example, when Ann choose the same book on successive weeks, her understanding changed in the intervening period. During this second reading of *The Tunnel* she again commented on the wolf but this time she had a confident understanding of pictorial metaphor: now she was sure that it was 'a tree shaped like a wolf.' She was also able to make explicit what in the previous week had remained unsaid: that what restored the brother to life was Rose's specific act of loving (see figure 26).

She threw her arms around the cold hard form, and wept. Very slowly, the figure began to change colour, becoming softer and warmer.

Figure 26 From *The Tunnel* by Anthony Browne, published by Julia MacRae Books

■ **Ann**   (*unprompted*) She cuddled him, first, then he turned into a
colour . . . and then (*pointing*) that, that and that . . . (*inaudible*)
. . . and then he comes all alive again.
VW   What is it that makes him come back to life?
Ann   Um, her cuddling him.
VW   Why does cuddling him make him come back to life?
Ann   Because, then, they like each other now.   ■

She tried also to explain to Sadie why the two endpapers were different.

■ **Ann**   (*indicating the opening endpaper*) This page, it's just the book.
And on this bit there's nothing. And the book's just there because
they don't like each other then. And then they lose the book . . .
(*inaudible*).   ■

I doubt if Sadie derived much insight from this rather garbled
explanation. But Ann was trying to work out something else. Her
reference to 'losing the book' indicates that she was working on a new
link: she still wanted to explain her original idea about reconciliation, but
she also wanted to link this somehow with the fact that the book had been
left abandoned outside the tunnel when Rose had gone in. But her words
fell apart and all she could say was:

■ **Ann**   (*looking at the final endpaper*) . . . the book and ball because they
like each other now.   ■

In many of his books, Anthony Browne's crowded and bizarre
illustrations are clues to his central theme. *The Tunnel* is full of imagery
associated with Red Riding Hood, and the numerous pigs in *Piggybook*[12]
are appropriate to the theme of male-piggery. In *Gorilla*[13] there is a
complex and delicate web of images and colour associated with the related
themes of loneliness, love and strength. In *Changes*[14] the surreal imagery is
eventually revealed as not surreal at all, but psychological – a complex and
serious 'image-play' on the father's remark that 'things were going to
change.'[15] But in other works his bizarre imagery is just bizarre. This can
be as much fun for a new reader but does not call into play such deeply
integrative processes as Ann had shown herself capable of when we shared
The Tunnel. Ann – and indeed all the others who chose them –

recognised that in these cases the meaning *is* the unexpectedness, and the shock of laughter that this induces is an appropriate response to the way surrealism blocks off interpretative readings. This is not 'reading for meaning' but learning to enjoy the *disruption* of meaning.

In *Look What I've Got!* [16], for example, the main theme is the come-uppance of the boaster, but the surreal pictorial jokes are only very tenuously linked with this. When I tried to direct Ann to the words, she did her best but with no sign of interest; you can't blame her really – there's little to say about them. Her animation – as always – was reserved for examining and commenting on the pictures. With Ann, the words were always an interruption to the main task. My tape of her sharing this with me (she was five then) recounts a string of exclamations, each indicating surprise: Look! – What's that? – Ducks! – There! – And there! – and a lot of laughter, and pointing. She speculated once or twice, but mostly her contributions were noticing signals. There are two woollen jumpers holding hands on a washing-line, and Ann simply pointed this out and laughed. That was all she could do since it is unlikely that the jumpers have any meaning beyond themselves (unless they are a pointed contrast with the unfriendliness of the boys). There was a lot of laughing – but we should not undervalue laughter; it always indicates some kind of recognition and is an implicit and usually social act of interpretation. She enjoyed noticing the flowers in the boot, the tree in a window, the man's tummy in another window, and the buttercup in the cow's nose. My attempts to invite an explicit interpretation were disregarded.

> ■ **VW**   What do you think a tree is doing in the window?
> **Ann**   I don't know.   ■

And that was that! But she did make one link: her sharp eye saw a graphic connection between the tiny football bouncing off a hedgehog and a big football bouncing off Sam's hairy head. (Though why there is so much hair in Anthony Browne's illustrations puzzles me!) The picture of the park was her favourite; she spent several minutes hunting out the details – a fish in a streetlamp, another being taken for a walk, and another being used as a golf-club, while a distant tree is fish-shaped and there is a fisherman wading in the ground. I wish I understood all these fishes; I did understand that the frog on the park-keeper's uniform is a pun (only because during National Service, I had frogs on my army uniform). But Ann was untroubled, content to delight in each new discovery. There was one pun which she did appreciate: that the only dog near the BEWARE OF THE DOG sign was a hot-dog. One of her discoveries was a small hair-line fault in the printing and two dots so minute that they could hardly be seen without a magnifying-glass; Ann was sure they meant something. Anthony Browne had made Ann into a post-modernist reader and taught her to find significance in every detail! She and Sadie often referred to 'Anthony Browne tricks' and they looked for them everywhere. Ann knew there was something odd about the pants on the washing-line, and when I explained about Y-fronts she instantly saw that the others had an X-front and a Z-front. 'Look,' she said, 'there's a bra with three . . .' Tactfully or mischievously, she left me to provide the noun. 'Cups?' I suggested carefully, and she agreed. She noticed that when Jeremy put on his gorilla-suit it is not only the old lady who is frightened, but also the small flower at the roadside, the distant hedge, the cow, the scarecrow ('a scared scarecrow'), the tree, the bobble on the lady's hat and the doll in her pocket (see figure 27). Ann was always thorough. She went all

"Grrrrrrrrrrrr!"

Figure 27
**From *Look What I've Got!*
by Anthony Browne,
published by Julia
MacRae Books**

through the book like this, and when she reached the final page with the animal-trees she sought out *The Tunnel* again so that she could compare it with the forest pictures she remembered from her reception days.

These weeks of book-sharing were exciting and illuminating – but there was a problem. There was in Ann a stubborn resistance to my attempts to interest her in the words on the page. All the other children I worked with at that period were, in their different ways, beginning to work at it, collaborating happily and predictably in the usual 'apprenticeship' activities, reinforced by their writing and the classteacher's work on phonics. But not Ann. She had all manner of ways of diverting my attempts to direct her attention to the words. It soon became apparent that she was not in the approved sense 'making any progress.' Her class teacher was becoming anxious. Ann had only a rudimentary grasp of phonic correspondences for single consonants, none at all for vowel sounds, and she seemed to have hardly any sight vocabulary at all. I had to stop joint sessions with her friends because the contrast between their reading and hers was so obvious.

The apprenticeship approach to reading depends on the learner's willingness to cooperate in a process of seduction. The child's attention must be drawn from the pictures to the words. It is usually, in my experience, effortless, because most children eventually develop an interest in the signs, if only because of the increasing amount of writing they are doing. But when this process did not happen, I found myself asking whether it was possible that a preoccupation with the syntax of pictures *obstructed* an understanding of the different syntax of sentences? Was it possible that when I insisted that Ann should concentrate on the linear fixity of words I was in danger of 'closing down' the interpretative and exploratory openness associated with her reading of pictures?

The contrast between Sadie and Ann was significant. Sadie's interest in the pictures was mostly literal and at first she had a rather stumbling and mechanical approach to reading words (see chapter 8). But she came through this period and became, so quickly that it seemed almost overnight, a confident and fluent reader. Ann, on the other hand, had her extraordinary ability to read pictures but remained unable to read the simplest and commonest words. It was especially depressing that, as time went on, she appeared to be losing her readiness to talk about pictures. I believe that for a while Ann was almost silenced by her awareness of failure.

This was a difficult period of about a year and a half. But we met every week, and Ann still chose her favourites. She never tired of *Rosie's Walk*, and she liked most of Satoshi Kitamura's picture books. She was fond of *Do Not Open*[17] and – like all the readers I have worked with – *Peace at Last.*[18] Long after her peers had moved to other books, Ann continued to choose *The Very Hungry Caterpillar*[19], *A Dark Dark Tale*[20], and *Let's Go Home, Little Bear.*[21] These books provided her with the reassurance of simple repetitive texts, but she showed no sign of what for so many new readers is a breakthrough – that imperceptible shift from 'reciting' to 'reading' familiar words. Her 'best favourite' was *Knock Knock Who's There?*[22], mostly because she and I read the parts, but also because the illustrations provide almost endless opportunities for discussion. If I wanted her to have a go at a particular book, she would do a deal provided we finished with *Knock Knock Who's There?*

There was no breakthrough with Ann, but slowly her reading did improve. I have a tape of her reading *Gorilla*[23] when she was six-and-a-half. She was still not a confident or fluent reader; she needed a lot of prompts and corrections, and she was thankful when I gave her a rest by reading a page myself. However, her amazing observation of detail had not diminished. She pointed out all the gorillas, of course, and observed that those on the lampshades in Hannah's bedroom are cheering triumphantly when *the* Gorilla comes to life. She asked why the kitchen picture had so much blue and white, and I explained that many people thought blue was a chilly colour. She made no response, but later, when Hannah and the Gorilla are eating, she very sensibly remarked that the reds make it a warm picture.

Generally, though, she showed little sign of deep interpretative reading. She did ask the central question about the absence at the heart of the book: 'Where's her mum?' she asked. But she did not develop this, and she showed no sign of seeing any connection between the Gorilla and the father. She came close to it once –

■ **VW**   Why has he got a banana sticking out of his pocket?
  Ann   I don't know. (*pause*) . . . The Gorilla likes bananas.   ■

But that was all. When I replayed this tape, I found I had asked seven
leading questions which might have prompted her to comment on
Hannah's loneliness, or the father's failure; and seven times Ann said in a
rather quavering voice, 'I don't know.' Was she just bored by my
questioning? Was there in her head a secret inner speech where her real
thinking was taking place? Or is it just possible – I do hope not – that, as
she came more under the influence of the words on the page, she
gradually lost her inventive and free-ranging openness to the pictures? [24]

There was on that occasion one more demonstration of her astonishing
memory for pictorial detail. There is a small illustration of a staircase, in
which there is a patch of red and a pair of dressing-gown tassles in one
corner of the frame. Ann knew that this indicated that Hannah had
rushed downstairs (see figure 28). She suddenly asked to have a look at

Figure 28   **From *Gorilla* by Anthony Browne, published by Julia MacRae
            Books**

The Tunnel, which she had not looked at for more than a year, and in which she remembered that Anthony Browne had employed a similar device. She found the forest illustration in which this occurs, pointed it out – and immediately spotted a gorilla's head *there* too, at the foot of the tree behind the frightened Rose. Neither of us had noticed that before.

In what was to be our last session, Ann chose what I believe is one of the wisest books ever made for young readers, *Mr Gumpy's Outing.* [25] It was a sensible choice; Ann probably knew that its quite simple text was one she could read with a genuine feeling of achievement. She did, in fact, read it quite accurately, and with the beginnings of fluency, pausing after each page to look at the pictures. Her first observation was that Mr Gumpy's house was the same as the house in *Granpa* and that John Burningham seemed to like wheelbarrows. Then – (see figure 29)

■ **Ann**   I hate dandelions . . . I *do* like them, the look of them, but I hate
         picking them.
  VW   Is that because their stalks are full of that white stuff?
  Ann   Yes. Yes . . . and when I suck my thumb that white stuff tastes . . . ■

Figure 29 From *Mr Gumpy's Outing* by John Burningham, published by Jonathan Cape

And later, looking at the cat with its straight tail –

■ **Ann**   Nearly always, I do tails wiggly . . . like that (demonstrates with her finger).   ■

And, on the foliage in the goat illustration –

■ **Ann**   Why has it got all black on there?
VW   I don't know . . . Shadows?
Ann   It might have been raining.   ■

These comments were what might be described as technical/aesthetic – about the visual appeal of dandelions, how to draw tails, and the use of a particular colour. And, amazingly, she made her first phonetic comment: she pointed at 'muck' and said, 'If that was a 'b' that would be buck.' In several hours of tapes, that was the only comment Ann had ever volunteered about any of the words! The words and pictures in *Mr Gumpy's Outing* exist in perfect balance; neither demand too much attention. Ann seemed to feel happy with this, liberated perhaps to react equally to both. There is no deeply-layered theme in it, though she came as close as one can get when she said, 'They all do what they're told not to.' Precisely!

With every other new reader I have had a feeling of achievement and gratification, even when progress was slow and uneven. But I could not quite shake off a suspicion that, for Ann, learning to read involved some kind of loss. I suppose it is reasonable to point out that a child so fascinated by images should not have been allowed to choose so many Anthony Browne books in which the words are so secondary to the pictures. If you want to teach a child to read, it could be argued, you should not provide books which subvert language. But it may have nothing to do with a particular picture book-maker. Could it be that the processes of trying to manage the syntax of sentences and the logic of letters did some kind of violence to Ann's ability to spin subtle narrative webs out of pictures? Or, to put it another way, that being required to learn to read for her was analogous to the old practice of forcing left-handed children to use their right hands?

161

I know it is more likely that, as she grew older, Ann preferred to keep her perceptions to herself simply because she had become more reticent or a little lazy – or because she had begun to suspect that talking about pictures was babyish. But suppose there *are* 'left-handed readers' in our classrooms. What then?

REFERENCES

1 Maurice Sendak, *Outside Over There*. London: Bodley Head, 1981.

2 Jane Doonan has, in fact, provided an answer in an absorbing article on 'Outside Over There' in *Signal 50* and *51*, May and September, 1986.

3 Jane Doonan, *Looking at Pictures in Picture Books*. Gloucester: Thimble Press, 1993.

4 Anthony Browne, *The Tunnel*. London: Julia MacRae Books, 1989.

5 I have written elsewhere about Ann's reading of *The Tunnel*. See, Morag Styles and Jane Drummond, *The Politics of Reading*. Cambridge: University of Cambridge and Homerton College, 1993, pp. 21–2.

6 Ann might also have responded subliminally to the window, which is shaped like a witch's hat.

7 To be precise, Anthony Browne is quoting Walter Crane's fairytale wolf, from his illustrated *Red Riding Hood*.

8 Jan Ormerod, *The Story of Chicken Licken*. London: Walker Books, 1985.

9 Morag Styles, Eve Bearne and Victor Watson (eds), *After Alice*. London: Cassell, 1992, p. 47.

10 Raymond Briggs, *The Snowman*. London: Hamish Hamilton, 1978.

11 Pat Hutchins, *Rosie's Walk*. London: Bodley Head, 1970.

12 Anthony Browne, *Piggybook*. London: Julia MacRae Books, 1986.

13 Anthony Browne, *Gorilla*. London: Julia MacRae Books, 1983.

14 Anthony Browne, *Changes*. London: Julia MacRae Books, 1991.

15 I know some adult readers find this book distressing; but I suspect that the boy is firmly in control of all these imagined changes, and is *making them happen*.

16 Anthony Browne, *Look what I've Got!* London: Julia MacRae Books, 1980.

17 Brinton Turkle, *Do Not Open*. New York: E. P. Dutton, 1981.

18 Jill Murphy, *Peace at Last*. London: Macmillan, 1980.

19 Eric Carle, *The Very Hungry Caterpillar*. New York and Cleveland: World Publishing Company, 1969.

20 Ruth Brown, *A Dark Dark Tale*. London: Andersen Press, 1981.

21 Martin Waddell, *Let's Go Home, Little Bear*. London: Walker Books, 1981.

22 Sally Grindley, illus. Anthony Browne, *Knock Knock Who's There?* London: Hamish Hamilton, 1985.

23 Op. cit.

24 We know that words can be evocative and magically suggestive too, but not probably if what excites you, to the exclusion of almost everything else, is *images*.

25 John Burningham, *Mr Gumpy's Outing*. London: Jonathan Cape, 1970.

Penny plain, tuppence coloured: reading words, and pictures

Helen Arnold

In the concluding chapter of *Talking Pictures*, Helen Arnold directly addresses the real books and reading schemes debate. Recognising the value that lies in structure and the need for explicit teaching about print, she shows why using picture books as the texts on which children learn to read is so important. By analysing the quality of the interaction between print and illustration in a random selection of recently published popular scheme books, she demonstrates why good picture books are superior. The former concentrate on pictures which reflect the printed text rather than enhance it, play games with it, tell another story, hint at added subtleties and all the other things that gifted illustrators do in picture books, as the writers in this book have tried to demonstrate. The chapter closes with the suggestion that some of the tenets of the philosophy behind reading schemes, structure, repetition, attention to print, phonic knowledge, could be put more systematically into practice in early years classrooms using picture books – not special ones commissioned to fit with new reading schemes which somehow never match the quality of the individual picture book, but those exceptional pictorial texts, some of which have been celebrated in these pages.

‘ Polonius: What do you read my Lord?
 Hamlet: Words, words, words.   ’
                                                        Hamlet: [Act 2 Scene II].

In this chapter I look at the relationships between the 'penny plain' words and the 'tuppence coloured' illustrations, in the context of the teaching of reading.

164

When Jeanne Chall wrote *Learning to Read: the Great Debate*[1], the great debate was centred on ways of teaching word recognition skills – either through phonic or whole-word recognition methods. Debates about reading have continued to rage across at least three continents ever since, with the goal posts changing, but the acrimony as fierce as ever. In this country now, the issues have become more fundamental, because they are based on ideology rather than methodology.

Not only have the goalposts changed, but so has the world, perhaps largely because of the explosion of communication systems. I see the debate now as, on one side, an acceptance that alphabetical print and image-making are inextricably intermingled in all forms of media. Advertisements and documentaries juxtapose words, sometimes spoken, sometimes written, with pictures, overlapping, simultaneous, dazzling and teasing eyes and ears. Pop song videos beam words, almost subliminally, on to the screen to emphasise aspects of the sound. The logo is a subtle mixture of picture and text, and even acronyms seem almost image-like. So all of us are less likely to read pages of uninterrupted text than ever before. But we do need to be able to relate the juxtaposed messages to each other, and this is not necessarily an easy option. Picture books are the interface between the visual media and printed text. They would therefore seem ideal for introducing children to the new literacy.

Not so for the opposing debaters. Rather than realising that new ways of communicating demand new methods of teaching, the slogan 'back to basics' encapsulates the outlook which looks for a return to the methodologies and resources of the past. Hypothetical 'falling standards' are blamed on the rejection of reading schemes, with all that implies.

Martin Turner's pamphlet *Sponsored Reading Failure*[2], a polemic against learning to read with 'real' books, has had a disproportionate influence in the last five years. He compares picture books unfavourably with phonically based reading schemes like *Language in Action*[3]. In a section entitled 'A word is worth a thousand pictures', Turner accepts the 'rich quality of illustrations in current children's literature', but as for the words –

‘ the language is becoming impoverished . . . picture-cues are poor indicators of what is contained in the text. Some nouns can be shown; verbs to a lesser extent; narrative structures require the wholesale adoption of highly schematic, stylised conventions (as in children's comics) to mimic language; and thoughts cannot be represented at all.   ’

He goes on to make a strange plea for the 'phonic emphasis' on teaching reading because of the

‘ deeper emotional layers of language, the fact that words have evolved with subtly varied usages through centuries of change. They are historical objects. A word which is a thousand years old, and has passed through a thousand mouths before our own, is worth a thousand pictures.   ’

I have quoted at length from Turner, partly to illustrate the passionate, but to me, illogical thinking which prompts him to make the false dichotomy between pictures and words. Words *are* intriguing, but not as objects in themselves. A word is intriguing because it is a collection of arbitrary signs which evokes innumerable associations used in the contexts of experience, of different varieties of text, in relationship to other representations of experience like pictures. A letter has no 'meaning', a word on its own has limited meaning, but a word in context is rich with meaning.

There is more behind the plea for 'back to basics' than Turner's preoccupation with phonics. The psychology of learning and teaching underlies the debate about 'real books' or 'reading schemes'.

Reading schemes are designed to be used in a certain way in classrooms. They are invariably linked to some form of grading, now less rigid, but still of fundamental importance. If the material is staged in small steps, it is intended to ensure success through positive reinforcement. The reinforcement comes from the teacher hearing the child read each book regularly, typifying a behaviourist approach to learning. It is no surprise to find that the earliest schemes were devised by psychologists. 'Teaching' comprises 'checking' and 'passing on' to the next book. The repercussions are obvious. Readers are extrinsically motivated; the urge is to move as quickly as possible on to the said 'next book' until the goal of being 'off the scheme' is reached. Parents may be invited to co-operate, but this has usually meant receiving from school the precise text which has to be read each night (to be checked yet again in school the next day).

The achievement of reading in early education has always been seen as more important than anything else. This is not because its functional and recreative values in the future are foreseen, but because it is the most easily recognised form of 'schooling' in the early years. Reading schemes have symbolised structure and progression. They have been the chief means of initiating children into a school culture which deliberately discards connections with the realities outside school. So the material must *ipso facto* exemplify the traditions of the past.

' It would appear more important in these kinds of lesson sequences for students to be in tune, culturally and intellectually, with the teacher . . . we could conclude that these are essentially lessons in school culture, and more particularly, lessons in how school knowledge is generated and transmitted.[4]   '

It is important to take the arguments of 'back to basics' seriously, and to admit that there may also be strong ideologies operating within the 'real books' camp. The belief that reading will inevitably follow from sharing books and looking at pictures is debatable. There must at some point be a recognition of the difference between pictorial representation and an arbitrary alphabetic system, and not all children are going to achieve this knowledge without direct teaching. My arguments in the rest of this chapter are centred round the belief that picture books are just as appropriate, if not more so, for giving children this awareness, and that we should try to discard preconceived notions of an outdated school culture and replace them with a new structure.

I attempt to do this in two ways; first by comparing reading schemes and picture books as objectively as possible to suggest what is offered by each, regardless of methodology. Then I suggest, perhaps controversially, some ways in which picture books may be used to further reading achievement.

I am not here so much concerned with the content of the books. This volume seethes with examples of the rich multilayeredness of picture books, and there are many critiques of the content of reading schemes elsewhere. I am concerned with the accessibility of the penny plain words themselves, and the way in which they relate to the illustrations helpfully or unhelpfully.

I selected a random sample of ten books from popular schemes, most of them recently published. In every case the pattern of the page is similar – a picture with accompanying text, usually complete on a single page, occasionally bridging a double-page spread. In the books for 'higher grades' the print takes up more of the page, and the type becomes smaller. The surprising thing to me was that, without exception, each picture illustrates *exactly* what is printed in the text. For example,

‹ Little Billy and Big Billy were tired. There was only one bed. "We'll share it" said Little Billy. "Yes" said Big Billy. "We'll cut it in half." So they cut the bed in half. [5] ›

Little Billy and Big Billy were tired. There was only one bed.

"We'll share it," said Little Billy.

"Yes," said Big Billy. "We'll cut it in half."

So they cut the bed in half.

Figure 30 From *Silly Billys* by Joy Cowley, published by Heinemann Educational

The picture shows the bed being cut exactly in half with a saw by the two Billys.

In *Max goes to School*[6] there is a difficulty as the children can see the friendly monster in the classroom whereas Miss Hobson can't. (We think of the innumerable ways in which picture book makers have illustrated similar situations.) Here the problem is solved by tracing Max in yellow line. Martin Turner would, of course, approve of such clear and direct picture-cues. I believe that either the pictures or the text are quickly going to become redundant for the reader (or, in the case of many scheme stories, both!).

As *Talking Pictures* shows constantly, in good picture books the text and illustrations relate quite differently, with a contrapuntal rather than an overlapping match. For example, in *Avocado Baby*[7] the first double-page spread has two pictures which are out of sequence. The first, alongside the text, shows Mr. and Mrs. Hargraves carrying their new baby in its carry-cot up to their front door. The second picture fills the page, with a flash-back to the mother in hospital with the new baby and visiting family, surrounded by gifts. Here Mrs. Hargraves is smiling gently, cradling her baby proudly.

The text reads

> ‘ The new baby was born and all the family were very pleased. Mr. and Mrs. Hargraves brought the baby home and it grew, but as they feared, it did not grow strong. Mrs. Hargraves found feeding the baby very difficult. It did not like food or want to eat much. ’

Very little of this text is directly illustrated. The events go well beyond the page, back to the previous page, where we have learnt that the Hargraves family is not strong, but who hope for a baby who is not weak, and on to the next page where the series of wordless pictures show the agonising and fruitless attempts to persuade the baby to feed. The smile on Mrs. Hargraves' face in hospital carries all the hidden doubts of past and future.

It can be argued that the complexities of 'reading' a picture book are far too great for beginning readers, and that the simple relationship between

Figure 31 From *Avocado Baby* by John Burningham, published by Jonathan Cape

pictures and text is the best way of showing young readers how words 'label' things in the world. But this is not true, even of the youngest child learning to talk. Words are part of emotional webs, and link with other experiences, just as *Avocado Baby* shows. They are not just labels.

Perry Nodelman in *Words about Pictures*[8], discusses the possibility of different brain functioning in the processing of words and pictures. The right and left hemispheres may operate two ways of seeing the world:

‹ Left-hemisphere consciousness is lineal, sequential, causal, focal, explicit and verbal — typical of Western 'rational' thought — and right-hemisphere consciousness is non-lineal, simultaneous, acausal, diffuse, tacit and spatial — typical of the 'intuitional' thought of so-called primitive societies. ›

He describes how in looking at a picture book 'pictures tend to be diffuse, words explicit'. But he agrees with Howard Gardner that the modes of consciousness cannot be easily separated: 'It is almost unthinkable that our "normal" minds should not utilise both halves of the brain'.

He concludes that 'the picture book is distinguished by the ways in which it takes advantage of such highly specialised relationships'. In reading and looking we are not necessarily interpreting in completely discrete ways, and we are certainly not just using words to label or describe what we see. So an exact replica of the picture in words or vice-versa does not mirror the way we reflect on experience. It is therefore not necessarily 'easier' to relate pictures and text in a reading scheme book than in a picture book.

The second aspect I want to touch on is the language used in both types of book. One of the most powerful reasons given for using reading schemes is that the readability is carefully monitored, words are graded and repeated, and the sentence structure is simple and unambiguous. We should also be able to see at a glance which methodology a particular scheme is espousing – for example, predominantly 'phonics' or 'look and say'.

Language in Action is one of the few schemes which adopts a strictly phonic approach: 'Meg, the peg-leg, has a fat cat, – has a fat cat in a sun hat'[9], so at least we know where we are. (*Language in Action* is now out of print.) 'Upside Down Harry Brown' (All Aboard Stage 5)[10] is an example of a recently published scheme:

> ' 'Harry Brown, Upside Down!'
> The school kids cried.
> The kids were the right way up,
> not like Harry Brown.
> Harry Brown was upside down! '

This is more difficult to classify. It flirts with a more recent approach to phonics[11] which places importance on recognising onset and rhyme, juxtaposing 'br-own' and 'd-own'. Frequently met function words (à la *Key Words to Literacy*) are also apparent ('were', 'was', 'right' 'cried') and there is repetition. Sentences are short – very short.

The Oxford Reading Tree (Stage 4)[12] *Come In* has fewer words to a page:

> Four children came to the house.
> They came to play with Chip.
> "Come in" said Chip.

The text seems to be using a methodology which rests on whole word recognition and retention. Any child trying to read phonically would have difficulties here: 'with', 'Chip' 'in', 'children' are the only words which can be easily 'sounded out', and even they need the knowledge of the consonant blend 'ch'.

At a later 'stage' Story Chest[13], the text remains short, but there is no apparent vocabulary control. Sentences are short, but words are long! – 'centimetre', 'hollered', 'shopkeepers', 'bad-mannered'.

Whatever the readability level, it is self-evident that these texts have in common a stilted, jerky awkward feel about them. Turner's description of picture book texts, quoted above ('narrative structures require the wholesale adoption of highly schematic, stylised conventions') seems entirely appropriate here!

If we compare the language of picture books on the same basic criteria we find surprisingly that the average word count in many books is similar, and that there is just as much repetition, alliteration, rhyme, and the same combination of words which are phonically regular with 'look and say' words. Many of the sentences are short, too. But here the similarities end. There is a far greater variety in sentence structure and more direct conversation. Many of the sentences are more accessible because they follow natural speech patterns. Some picture book authors work deliberately to help children towards awareness of language. The whole plot of Pat Hutchins' *The Surprise Party*[14] centres round mistaken hearing. 'I'm having a party' is misheard as 'hoeing the parsley'; 'going to sea' is heard as 'climbing a tree' and so on, throughout the book. Anthony Browne's speech bubbles in *Zoo*[15] invite 'sounding out with expression' – 'GGGRRR! !', 'Uh-uh-uh-uh!'

There therefore seems little basis in using reading schemes for teaching reading because they have simpler or more carefully chosen language.

Reference to *The Surprise Party* leads me to my final section, in which I argue that it is legitimate to use the words of picture books to help readers master 'the basic skills'.

Victor Watson[16] wonders whether reading words demands a different kind of thinking from reading pictures, and earlier in this chapter I discussed the possible influences of the two sides of the brain. The thinking may be radically different, but I do not think so. Other factors may account for delay in some children in achieving reading mastery. In picture books the 'penny plain' of the words are usually in black and white, not so noticeable as the 'tuppence coloured' of the striking illustrations. We all tend to pay initial attention to the pictures, and indeed as adults to delight in the way that children seize on small details almost simultaneously with gaining a holistic view. We naturally, therefore, work with them from the pictures first, doing all the right things, motivating through interest, encouraging prediction, inviting links with personal experience and emotional response, using the picture as a trigger. All this is right, but it may sometimes be at the expense of the text, which is read aloud once or twice, but not necessarily explored in the same depth as the pictures. A transcript of a lesson given by a teacher sharing a Big Book with six-year-olds (*One Cold Wet Night*[17]) was categorised by researchers. They counted the ways in which the teacher directed the group towards answering her questions. From forty directives, nineteen referred to the picture (for example 'Just have a look at the picture . . . forget the words for a moment'.) Only two directives referred specifically to the words ('it said in the book' . . .' remember what is said in our story'). Eve Gregory[18] found similar emphases in her research with a differentiation between children who were already readers, and who tended to refer the teacher back to the text, and those who were encouraged to talk more vaguely about their own experiences.

It is vital that the 'whole' book is appreciated, and *Talking Pictures* has repeatedly exemplified the intelligence and involvement shown in child responses, but I do not think this enjoyment would be lessened by paying close attention to the 'penny plain' words. Two things help us here, and the first is, for me, the prop of a different approach to teaching reading based upon the ancient method of repetition, but not repetition of single words. Picture books bear endless revisiting. We do not need hundreds of carefully graded banal texts which have to be slavishly followed. We could structure the learning round fewer books, allowing children to come to know them from many aspects. The books would become possessions. They would even bear learning by heart without becoming boring.

The second thing that helps is that children already apply many of the skills they need for reading words to the pictures. They search for details, they see patterning from page to page, they put pictures together into a sequence (as Morag Styles[19] points out). To read words may be more difficult, because the symbols are arbitrary, but the processes do not seem to me so very different.

The National Curriculum may not be explicitly friendly to picture books, but at least it does not specify the use of reading schemes, and its selection of literature suggested at Key Stage 1 is largely picture books. I suggest that the 'Key Skills' can be covered by using the text of picture books in a variety of ways, with the caveat that we start and finish with the whole story. We could, for instance, as some teachers already do, make card games of words from stories to encourage phonic and graphic knowledge. We could cut paragraphs into phrases and give one to each player, inviting them to physically 'put it all together' (Grammatical Knowledge). And as for Contextual Knowledge, there are myriads of activities for all ages. Nodelman[20] describes how he asked children and adults to

> ‘ record the stories that occur to them as they experience only the pictures of picture books . . . and read the texts . . . without the accompanying pictures. ’

He found that readers rarely managed to equate with the originals, arriving at a 'surprising variety of different stories'. There are great possibilities here in helping children to appreciate the surprising relationships between the pictures and words of the originals.

It may seem like sacrilege to dissect the language in this way. Nobody however would be against focusing on the text by asking groups to tape-record a story with sound effects, to interview each other in role, to turn the story into role-play. I am suggesting that we draw attention to the words of the books in different ways and at different levels, continually

174

going back to the same books. This would involve buying small sets of texts, and could also involve older children devising activities for younger readers.

The written language, therefore, can be a focus of special attention. It would be interesting for older readers, for instance, to compare Anthony Browne's earlier writing with his later books – from the sparse authorial voice of *Through the Magic Mirror*[21]

> ' An invisible man passed by.
> On the corner was an easel. On the easel was
> a painting of a painting of a painting . . .   '

to the character as narrator, exploiting all the nuances of a child's sentence structure and vocabulary, in *Zoo*[22].

> ' My brother thumped me, so I kicked him
> and we wrestled for a bit, then Dad told
> me off . . .   '

and the wonderful Philip Marlowe-type pastiche of *King Kong*[23] –

> ' That was why Denham was walking the streets of New York, looking for
> the right face for his film, the face of Beauty.   '

So the text begins to become as 'tuppence coloured' as the pictures. The words are as rich as the illustrations.

We need to remember, on the one hand, that

> ' the potentially enabling functions of literacy can be limited or even
> reversed by current instructional materials and by the kind of activities
> that surround those materials in classrooms. That is, the uses to which
> schools may put literacy can counter the very consciousness that many
> educators take to be the richest offering of the written word[24]   '

and believe, on the other hand, what a postgraduate student recently discovered from her encounters with picture books:

175

❛ Personal experience tells me that the best books are those in which a single phrase can open up a new universe, which inspire a thirst to read more, and where each reading yields something new. So multi-layered texts are 'ageless' because of all they offer the reader, including the child reader.[25] ❜

Penny Plain and Tuppence Coloured work their magic together.

REFERENCES

1 Jeanne Chall, *Learning to Read: the Great Debate*. New York: McGraw Hill 1967, 1983.

2 Martin Turner, *Sponsored Reading Failure*. Warlingham: IPSET Education Unit, 1990.

3 Joyce Morris, *Language In Action*. London: MacMillan Education, 1974.

4 Carolyn Baker and Peter Freebody, *Children's First School Books*. Oxford: Basil Blackwell, 1989, pp. 182.

5 Joy Cowley, *Silly Billys*. Sunshine Books 3. London: Heinemann Educational, 1988.

6 Ted Wragg, *Max Goes to School*. Flying Boot 4. Walton on Thames: Thos. Nelson and Sons, 1994.

7 John Burningham, *Avocado Baby*. London: Jonathan Cape, 1982.

8 Perry Nodelman, *Words about Pictures: the Narrative Art of Children's Picture Books*. Georgia: University of Georgia Press, 1988, pp. 198.

9 Joyce Morris, op. cit. Peg-leg Meg Level 1

10 Martin Waddell, *Harry Brown Upside Down*. All Aboard Aylesbury: Ginn, 1994.

11 Usha Goswami and Peter Bryant, *Phonological Skills and Learning to Read*. Hove: Lawrence Erlbaum Associates, 1990.

12 Roderick Hunt, *Come In*. Oxford Reading Tree 4. Oxford: Oxford University Press, 1986.

13 Michael Yorke, *Loud Shout Lilli*. Story Chest. Leeds: Arnold-Wheaton, 1987.

14 Pat Hutchins, *The Surprise Party*. Puffin Books, 1970.

15 Anthony Browne, *Zoo*. London: Julia MacRae Books, 1992.

16 Victor Watson, This volume: Chapter 11

17 Carolyn Baker and Peter Freebody, op. cit. pp. 158

18 Eve Gregory, 'What Counts as Reading in the Early Years?' in *British Journal of Educational Psychology 63*, pp. 214–30

19 Morag Styles, This volume: Chapter 2

20 Perry Nodelman, 1988, page 193 op. cit.

21 Anthony Browne, *Through the Magic Mirror*. London: Hamish Hamilton, 1976.

22 Anthony Browne, *Zoo*, 1992, op. cit.

23 Anthony Browne, *King Kong* 1994, op. cit.

24 Carolyn Baker and Peter Freebody, 1989, op. cit. pp. 205.

25 Caroline Thomas, 'What I have learned about children's texts and reading'. Unpublished assignment: Homerton College, 1995.

Conclusion – a final word

Talking Pictures has been concerned with several different constituencies. One continuous thread has been the voices of young readers as they teach us the significance of picture books and wonder why adults ask obvious questions about something they take for granted – making meaning and taking pleasure in pictorial texts. Then there are the teachers, delicately treading a careful path in their desire to help children become fluent readers as early as possible, and their knowledge that clumsy interference could spoil the growing bond between apprentice readers and their chosen texts.

Behind the scenes are parents who are often aware of the love affair between children and picture books, but are confused by the clamorous voices in the public domain, asserting that young pupils must learn to read with phonics or reading schemes, and that picture books are suitable only for the early rungs of the ladder to reading success. Beyond them are the powerful voices of the government whose backward-looking ideology has been so effective that they have almost entirely excluded the role of pictorial texts in learning to read from the latest version of Reading in the English National Curriculum'. But this is madness. Whatever methodology of teaching reading schools espouse, considerable time is devoted to the use of illustrations in early literacy, *and* phonics, *and* whole-word recognition. They are not mutually exclusive! We need to remember that in earlier versions of the National Curriculum for English, visual literacy was properly reflected and the value of picture books acknowledged. As a genre, the picture book has pride of place in virtually every early years classroom; for children younger than six, *picture books constitute literature.* What then, apart from adherence to a narrow, ill-informed viewpoint, or a desire to appease back-bench Tory MPs furious about the government line on Europe, has caused this vital aspect of literacy to receive such a low profile in the new English document? It certainly isn't argument or educational evidence.[1]

Wisely, illustrators take little notice of raging debates about reading, and get on with creating books that will excite, tease, reassure, amuse and absorb young readers. Their voices are not often heard, but in *Talking Pictures* we have coaxed one of the finest picture book authors, Shirley Hughes, into articulating her intentions when she illustrates books for children. And we have paid attention to the written comments of others, such as Sendak and Browne, and located the current 'golden age' of picture books in a historical context.

A new concern about reading that has entered the public arena is the so-called 'great literature versus popular culture' debate. For many years now, the truism that television is bad for children, ruins their reading habits and is full of low-level programmes, has had wide currency. Journalists, politicians and others can often be heard deploring this trend, but there is little evidence to support it. One suspects a heavy dose of nostalgia by the intellectual elite comes into it, of rainbow-coloured days gone by when children loved to read the classics! The fact is that most children didn't; most, like me, picked up the reading habit from Enid Blyton, if we were lucky, and devoured every comic we could lay our hands on. Far more children learn to read effectively now than thirty years ago, and there seems some evidence in booming sales of fiction and poetry that far more people are choosing to read. Television, indeed, is often the stimulus for best-seller status of the 'classics' – *Middlemarch, Persuasion, Martin Chuzzlewit* are recent examples from adult fiction: the same is true for children's classics, such as *The Borrowers*.

As for television, there are many quality programmes for children who also watch popular media texts with intelligence and discrimination. Ask a sophisticated six-year-old viewer to read the semiotic of a favourite 'ad' and you'll see! Many teachers are aware that the comic is one of the best and most motivating genres for teaching reading, but this is too unsettling for those with fixed views of what children should read and how they should learn to do it. And, of course, the fact that children take such pleasure from these texts, is enough to convince some commentators that they must be harmful.

More importantly for the scope of this book, the sophisticated skills of visual literacy taught by television and developed by reading comics and picture books, are largely ignored. Most adults fail to understand the primacy of new literacies, including the visual, which will be vital for young people if they are to cope successfully with the changing world of the twenty-first century. And how is the curriculum responding to the computer revolution, the information superhighway, CD ROM, multimedia society? By going back to basics! By the introduction of a traditional curriculum which was supposed to have served us so well in the past! By testing narrow skills and failing to appreciate the intellectual potential of, among other things, visual and media texts!

As for the notion of 'great literature', the picture book texts which are considered 'classics' by adults – *Where the Wild Things Are, Granpa, Gorilla, Dogger, Angry Arthur, Not Now, Bernard, The Jolly Postman, Sunshine, The True Story of the Three Little Pigs* and literally hundreds more – are the same texts which children themselves adore and choose to re-read. For once, popularity and quality are indistinguishable. All the artists we have chosen to feature in *Talking Pictures* and all the individual picture books that have been discussed, we hold to be examples of the finest literature for children by any criteria that could be devised.

Talking Pictures has attempted to demonstrate and celebrate the cleverness children show when they read pictures, read between the lines and pictures, read layers of meaning, read a wide range of cultural references, cross-refer to other texts, fill in the gaps and generally handle various shades of complexity with apparent ease. They reveal how children imagine, wish, dream, quarrel, speculate and wonder with these texts. Some writers have tried in various ways to slow down the reading process, so that it can be examined in detail. Others have opened a window on the growing understandings of how children discover that print and illustrations work together. Another slant has been to show the range of knowledge and the sophisticated concepts that children are capable of mastering when genuinely engaged in reading picture books of their own choosing, and to credit the intellectual feat required to interpret complex pictorial texts. Our evidence comes from children who are usually aged six or younger, ordinary children, not specially gifted ones, though it has to be admitted that the classrooms we used were those with rich and positive reading environments. We watch children grappling with powerful themes and ideas and we observe closely the early stages of reading.

Talking Pictures also seeks to acknowledge and lay out for inspection *why* picture books are such enthralling texts. It is their very complexity and multilayeredness which gives them appeal. We are dealing with artifacts which not only fascinate children and help them learn to read; we have also ranged across many disciplines, including fine art, literature, media education and reading pedagogy.

Whereas other popular forms enjoyed by children are only tolerated by adults, picture books are as intellectually engrossing to adults as to children. We make no apologies for returning to the same texts and authors over and over again and for considering them in the light of contemporary theory. This was partly deliberate to give coherence to a book with different contributors, and partly because these are some of the texts we love ourselves and know that children return to, again and again. Nor do we apologise for giving pride of place to the operation of humour in picture books. By amusing their readers, picture books attract, engage and eventually hook them. To get the maximum fun, they have to be examined closely and worked at. That is an early reading lesson. Children quickly become skilful at reading the multifarious devices used by different humorists. And humour is sometimes a way of softening harsh issues and making painful things bearable.

If we have done nothing else, we hope that the teachers, parents, students, artists academics and children who have been doing the talking about pictures in this book, will have convinced the reader that visual literacy is a vital skill and that picture books offer the first steps towards enjoyment of literature, critical literacy, artistic education and independent, wide-ranging readings. Texts that can do all these things and are desirable to a young readership demand to be taken seriously.

Notes

1 Although picture books are the chosen genre of SATs at KS1 and are mentioned as suitable reading matter for that age group, visual literacy has been cut out of the key skills section on learning to read in the 1995 version of English in the National Curriculum.

Index

Aesop's Fables 17
Ahlberg, Allan & Janet 102, 104, 109, 111, 137–8
Alberti, Leon 110
Album de Caricatures 18
Alderson, Brian 6, 7, 16, 17
Aldo 26, 121
Alfie 74–5
Alice's Adventures in Wonderland 37, 103, 105–6
All Aboard 171
All Join In 141
Ally Sloper's Half-Holiday 19
Angry Arthur 36, 67–8, 93, 118–19, 180
Annie Rose 74–5
Anno, Mitsumasa 64–6
Anno's Journey 64–6
Ardizzone, Edward 19, 24
Art and Illusion: A Study in the Psychology of Pictorial Representation 18
Art of Illustration 1750–1900, The 8
art history 61–70
Asterix 19
Avocado Baby 169–70

Babes in the Wood, The 11
Baker, Carolyn 167
Beano, The 123–35
Bear Goes to Town 42
Bear Hunt 109
Bennett, Charles 16, 17
Bewick, Thomas 24
bi-lingual readers 136–44
Big Baby, The 28
Blackburn, H. 17
Bocklin, Arnold 35
Book of Nonsense, The 12
Borrowers, The 179
Briggs, Raymond 19–20, 26
Bromley, Helen 66
Browne, Anthony 26, 35, 37, 40, 42, 43, 50–55, 63, 92, 97, 102, 104, 106, 108, 109, 113–17, 121, 146, 147–51, 152–5, 159–60, 161, 172, 175, 179
Burningham, John 26, 35, 80–99, 104, 106, 108, 110, 121
Busch, Willhelm 18, 19
Buzz-a-Buzz, or the Bees 18

Caldecott, Randolph 6, 17–18, 24
Caldecott, Randolph: a Personal Memoir of His Early Art Career 17–18
Caldecott and Co.: Notes on Books and Pictures 15
caricature 16–20, 54
Carroll, Lewis 18, 103
Chall, Jeanne 165
Changes 106, 154
chapbooks 9–12

Children's Books in England: Five Centuries of Social Life 9
Children's First School Books 167
Children's Illustrated Books 13
Chips 19
Chocolate Wedding, The 119–20
Cinderella 11, 32, 48, 104
Cinderella [toy theatre] 13
Cinderumpelstiltskin 57, 58
Cock Robin 11
Come away from the water, Shirley 35, 94–7
Comic Adventures of Old Mother Hubbard, The see *Mother Hubbard*
Comic Alphabet, A 14
Comic Cuts 19
Comic Multiplication, A 14
comic strip 16–20, 36, 107, 123–35, 166, 179
Crane, Walter 24, 44, 162
Criticism, Theory and Children's Literature 99
Crowquill, Alfred 16, 17
Cruikshank, George 16

Dame Wonder's Transformations 14
Dark, Dark Tale, A 158
Darton, F.J. Harvey 9
Darton, William 11
Diverting History of John Gilpin see *John Gilpin*
Do Not Open 158
Dogger 75, 180
Don Quixote 66
Doonan, Jane 34, 41, 61, 146, 162
Doyle, Richard 16, 17, 24
Dulac, Edmund 75

Each Peach Pear Plum 105, 108, 110–11, 137–8, 141, 142
Early Children's Books and their Illustration 13
Egoff, Sheila 23
Elegy on Mrs Mary Blaize 12
Elmer 105
Enchantment in the Garden 75–8
English Children's Books, 1600–1900 8
Enormous Turnip, The 116

Fables of Aesop, The 11
Fairy Tale Scenic Books 15
Faithless Parrot, The 17
Father Christmas 20
Feaver, William 12, 15
flap-books 14, 137, 140
Fox, Carol 53, 58
Fred 125
Freebody, Peter 167
Frog Prince Continued, The 31, 104, 109–10
Frog Who Would A-Wooing Go, The 17

Fungus the Bogeyman 20
Funny Pips 19

Ganly, Helen 61–3
Gardner, Howard 171
Gem, The 19
Gentleman Jim 20, 26
Goldsmith, Oliver 12
Gombrich, E. 18
Gorilla 109, 141, 154, 158–9, 180
Goscinny, René & Uderzo, Albert 19
Gottlieb, J.H. 13
Graham, Judith 25, 83, 110
Granpa 25, 26, 80–99, 110, 121, 160, 180
Graphic, The 18, 19
Greedy Jem 17
Green, J.K. 13
Greenaway, Kate 24
Gregory, Eve 141, 142, 173

Hansel and Gretel 32, 104, 150
Hansel and Gretel [Anthony Browne] 35
harlequinades 14
Harris, John 11, 12
Haunted House 31, 42
Heath, Shirley Brice 110, 141
Hergé 19
Hill, and the Rock, The 105
History of Children's Book Illustration, A 6–7
Hobyahs, The 138–9, 141, 143
Hughes, Arthur 24
Hughes, Shirley 19, 36, 38, 49, 54, 71–9, 80, 107, 179
Hunt, Peter 26, 32, 35, 99
Hutchins, Pat 80, 172

I Hate my Teddy Bear 35
Inkpen, Mick 141, 142–3
intertextuality 3, 34, 36, 55–8, 66, 102–11, 121, 124, 126, 133–4, 140–1

Jack the Giant Killer 11
Jack the Giant Killer [toy theatre] 13
Jack's Bean Problem 57, 59
Jasper the Cat 141
Jasper's Beanstalk 143
Jeremiah in the Dark Woods 101–2
John Gilpin 12, 14
Johnson, Steve 31–2, 104
Jolly Christmas Postman, The 36, 105
Jolly Postman, The 103, 105, 180
Jyoti's Journey 61–3

Katie's Picture Show 104
Keeping, Charles 66–7
Key Words to Literacy 171
King Kong 175
Kipper 142–3
Kipper's Toybox 141
Kirsty Knows Best 97, 119
Kitamura, Satoshi 35, 36, 67–8, 108, 118–19, 148
Knock Knock Who's There? 109, 116, 158

Language in Action 171
Learning to Read: the Great Debate 165
Leech, John 16, 17
Leeson, Robert 11

Let's Go Home, Little Bear 158
Lewis, David 23, 32–3, 37, 80, 89
Lily Takes a Walk 35, 40
Lion, The Witch and the Wardrobe, The 135
Little Folks Living Nursery Rhymes in Moving Pictures 15
Little Pretty Pocket-Book, A 12
Little Rabbit Foo Foo 102, 108
Little Red Riding Hood 57, 66, 154, 162
Little Red Riding Hood [Walter Crane] 44
Little Red Running Shorts 57
Look Out, He's Behind You! 140, 143
Look What I've Got! 155
Lullaby Hullaballo 141
Lulu and the Chocolate Wedding 36
Lulu and the Flying Babies 119

Magnet, The 19
Man, The 20, 26
Max Goes to School 169
Mayhew, James 104
McKee, David 35, 102, 104, 105, 108
media texts 105, 165, 179
Meek, Margaret 23, 25, 30, 103, 105
Meggendorfer, Lothar 15
Millet, Jean François 65
Monet, Claude 106
Moonlight 107
Moss, Elaine 8
Moss, Geoff 33, 34, 36, 38
Mother Hubbard 11, 12
Mr Gumpy's Outing 85, 98–100, 116, 160–1
Muir, Percy 8, 13, 14, 15, 17
multi-layeredness 3, 64–5, 168, 180–1
Murphy, Jill 80, 158

narrative painting 71–9
Negotiation as a Critical Factor in Learning to Read in a Second Language 140
Newbery, John 12
Nodelman, Perry 170, 174
Not Now Bernard 35, 105, 141, 180

Oi! Get Off Our Train! 106
Old Mother Hubbard see *Mother Hubbard*
Old Nurse's Book of Rhymes, The 17
One Bear at Bedtime 141
One Cold Wet Night 173
Ormerod, Jan 107, 151
Otten, Charlotte 23
Outside Over There 26, 146, 172

panoramas 14
parody 55, 56, 58, 126
Peace at Last 80, 158
peep shows 13
phonic knowledge 2, 165–6, 171, 174
picture sheets 18
picturebooks, history of 5–22
Pienkowski, Jan 31
Piggybook 26, 63, 154
Pinocchio 66
Plumb, J.H. 13
pointillism 65
postmodernism 32–5, 38, 80–1, 97–9
Potter, Beatrix 14, 24
Princess and the Bowling Ball, The 57

Princess and the Pea, The 57
Private Eye 126
Propp, Vladimir 58
Prose and the Passion, The 44
Punch 16, 17
Pyatt, Lucy 41, 43

Rackham, Arthur 24, 75
reading schemes 2, 24, 165–76
'real books' 24, 166–7
Red Riding Hood see *Little Red Riding Hood*
Robinson Crusoe 9
Robinson, Charles 24
Robinson, W. Heath 24
Roger Rabbit 38
Rosie's Walk 25, 35, 80, 151, 158

Schnurrdibur, oder die Bien 18, 19
Scieszca, Jon 31–2, 34, 36, 55–8, 59, 68–70, 104
Sendak, Maurice 15, 19, 23, 24, 26, 35, 41–5, 61, 63–4, 179
Sesame Street 66
Shepard, Ernest 24
Silly Billys 168–9
Simmonds, Posy 36, 125
Sing a Song for Sixpence: the English Picture Book Tradition and Randolph Caldecott 6, 7
Sleeping Beauty 112
Slythe, R.M. 8
Smith, Frank 103
Smith, J.A. 13
Smith, Lane 34, 55–8, 59, 68–70
Snow White and the Seven Dwarfs 32, 104
Snowman, The 20, 26, 38, 151
Soloman, S.J. 79
Spencer, Margaret *see* Meek, Margaret
Sponsored Reading Failure 165–6
Stinky Cheese Man, The 34, 36, 55–8, 59
Story Chest 172
Story of a Fierce Bad Rabbit, The 14
Story of Chicken Licken, The 151
Story of Miss Moppet, The 14
Struwwelpeter 12
Styles, Morag 25, 174
Sunshine 107, 180
Surprise Party, The 172, 173

Teichler, Lynda 38

Tenniel, Sir John 18, 105–6
Thomas, Anabel 107–9
Thomas, Caroline 176
Through the Looking Glass 18
Through the Magic Mirror 106, 175
Through the Window 66–7
Tin-Pot Foreign General and the Old Iron Woman, The 20
Tintin 19
Tom Hickathrift 11
Tom Thumb 11
Töpffer, Rodolphe 18, 19
Tortoise and the Hair, The 58
Toucan Toucan 105
toy theatres 13
Tristram Shandy 57
True Story of the Three Little Pigs, The 34, 55–6, 68–70, 180
Tunnel, The 25, 43, 113–17, 147–51, 152–5, 157, 159–60
turn-up books 14
Turner, Martin 165–6, 169, 172

Unlucky Wally 20
Up and Up 36, 38–9, 80, 107

Very Hungry Caterpillar, The 158
Visitors Who Came to Stay, The 26, 108
vista books 13

Walk in the Park, A 40
Waterland, Liz 25
Watson, Victor 25, 43, 173
We Are All in the Dumps with Jack and Guy 41–3
Wells, Gordon 104
Whalley, J.I. & Chester, T.R. 6–7, 16, 17
When the Wind Blows 20, 26
When We Were Young: Two Centuries of Children's Book Illustration 12
Where the Wild Things Are 42, 63–4, 180
Where's Julius? 25, 37
Willy the Champ/Willy the Wimp 50–5
Words About Pictures 170
Wyeth, N.C. 24

zigzag books 14
Zoo 26, 172, 175

Young readers consulted

Alison 38–40
Ann 43–4, 80–99, 112–16, 119, 145–62
Ashley 38–40
Christina 106
Christopher 139–40
Claire 37
Hannah 140
Holly 38–40
Isaac 123–35
Jodie 137, 139, 140
Jonathan 101–2, 108
Justin 27–8, 31–2
Kate 31–2

Katy 137, 138, 141
Lucy 38–40
Madeleine 106
Matthew 105
Momahl 136–43
Rashid 30–1, 42
Ryan 38–40
Sadie 80–99, 112–22, 146, 152–7
Simon 37
Thomas 106
Tom 28–30
Wong Lee 27–8